Perspectives on
Attributional Processes

Perspectives on Attributional Processes

John H. Harvey
Vanderbilt University

Gifford Weary
Ohio State University

With an Invited Chapter by
Ben Harris
Vassar College

wcb

Wm. C. Brown Company Publishers
Dubuque, Iowa

Consulting Editor
Hal Sigall

Copyright © 1981, by Wm. C. Brown Company Publishers

Library of Congress Catalog Card Number: 80-53438

ISBN 0-697-06637-1

Printed in the United States of America

This book is dedicated to *Shay,
Beckett, P. T.* and other
such contributors.

Contents

Preface

We have written this book especially for persons who have had some prior interest in the literature on attributional processes and who wish to gain further perspective on this area of work. We have tried to emphasize ideas and approaches that seem to have durability and that will influence in a substantial way the future of attribution theory and research. In this vein, we believe that our particular emphasis may reflect developments in the attribution domain during much of the 1980s.

In this book, our coverage of work on attributional processes has been carefully selected. Overall, we have presented surveys of major foundation work produced in the 1950s, 1960s and early 1970s, together with discussions of more contemporary work, and a touch of assessment of the future of attribution work. In the first three chapters we have reviewed basic works and early advances in the field, as well as critical analyses of these approaches. In Chapters 4 through 7, we have surveyed applications of attributional analyses to the development of attribution of causality and responsibility, attributions of freedom and control, and in the development and treatment of maladaptive behavior. We are pleased to call the reader's attention to Chapter 4, by Ben Harris, an invited contribution on developmental aspects of attribution. We believe that this chapter provides an important complement to other discussions in the book and that it represents one of the most comprehensive and contemporary surveys of the development of attribution available in the literature. In Chapter 8, we present our view of theoretical and empirical directions and issues which are emerging in attribution work and which seem likely to be prominent throughout much of the 1980s.

We have tried to write this book so that it may be used in basic courses and seminars at both undergraduate and graduate levels. Further, we believe that the book may be used as a supplementary source in advanced, and perhaps some introductory, courses in social-personality and clinical psychology that emphasize attribution research.

While the work is indeed the product of a collective effort, Weary is responsible for Chapters 6 and 7, Harvey for Chapters 2, 3, and 5. We are equally responsible for Chapters 1 and 8.

Finally, we wish to express our gratitude to the people who helped us complete this project during the last twenty months. We are especially grateful to Harold Sigall and William Ickes who read and provided detailed commentary on the entire manuscript. In particular, we are grateful to the helpful editors and staff at Wm. C. Brown Publishers, particularly Susan J. Soley, and to our hard-working and accomplished typist-editor Ms. Connie Dyer-Covert.

John H. Harvey
Gifford Weary
January, 1981

Perspectives on Attributional Processes

Foundations

Introduction to Basic Attribution Theories

1

We interpret other people's actions and we predict what they will do under certain circumstances. Though these ideas are usually not formulated, they often function adequately. They achieve in some measure what a science is supposed to achieve: an adequate description of the subject matter which makes prediction possible (Heider, 1958, p. 5).

Attribution theory in social psychology began with Fritz Heider's (1944; 1958) seminal analyses of how people perceive and explain the actions of others. How one person thinks and feels about another person, how one perceives another, what one expects another to do or think, how one reacts to the actions of another—these were some of the phenomena with which Heider was concerned. It is important to note that his early analyses of social perception and phenomenal causality represent more of a general conceptual framework about commonsense, implicit theories people use in understanding the underlying causes of events they observe in their daily lives, than a set of systematic hypotheses and empirical findings. Perhaps for this reason, the value of Heider's work was not fully appreciated until the mid-1960s when Edward Jones, Harold Kelley, and their colleagues developed, largely from Heider's ideas, more systematic statements on attributional processes.

Thus, attribution theory is a relatively new research area in social psychology. Work in this area, however, already has become quite extensive. In fact, for a span of years in the mid-1970s as much as fifty percent of the articles in major journals concerned attributional processes. Moreover, the reader of this book will observe that attributional analyses have been applied to a number of phenomena. For example, there are attributional analyses of aggression (Dyck & Rule, 1978), helping (Ickes & Kidd, 1976), attraction (Regan, 1978), learned helplessness and depression (Abramson, Seligman, & Teasdale, 1978), and close relationships (Orvis, Kelley, & Butler, 1976). These applications illustrate the potential breadth of theorizing about people making causal inferences and forming impressions of others in a variety of social settings.

While this book is about perspectives on attribution theory and research and while we at times will refer to "attribution theory," we would like to point out that there is no monolithic theory in this domain of work. As soon will become evident to the reader, there are no well-accepted singular sets of assumptions or hypotheses, nor are there general conclusions concerning attributional processes that are tied together in a coherent logical network. Rather, there are several theoretical approaches to causal attributional processes, each of which has some similarities to and differences from the others. In addition to these attribution conceptions which are concerned primarily with the *process* of making an attribution, there are a number of analyses that are concerned primarily with the *consequences* of arriving at a given attribution. Kelley (1978) has termed these latter analyses attributional theories and has commented, "That's what most of the research is about—attribution-based theories of emotion, achievement, motivation, affiliation, helping, revenge, equity" (p. 375). Indeed, we have already noted the diverse and extensive phenomena to which attribution conceptions have been applied. In this book, we will examine both the concept of attribution and attributional theories; however, the reader should not be mislead into believing that there is more theoretical coherence in this area than there really is.

In the section below, we will inquire further about the definition of attribution and about why attributions are made. Next, we will review early basic attribution analyses provided by Heider (1958), Jones and Davis (1965) and Kelley (1967). Other important work on basic attributional processes has been done by Bem (1965; 1972) and also will be reviewed.

Definition and Central Features

What is an attribution? An attribution is an inference about why an event occurred or about a person's dispositions. As we shall discuss later in this chapter, we may make attributions about our own dispositions and experiences just as readily as we make attributions about others. Hence, attributions may be perceptions and inferences about others or about self.

As a way of illustrating the meaning of this concept, consider a situation in which two people have just met at a party and are subtly probing whether or not they want to get to know one another further. The male says that he has just broken off a two-year relationship with a female. He says that he terminated the relationship because (1) the other woman was too dependent on him, (2) he could not take his eyes off other women, (3) they had very different hygenic habits, and (4) he did not get along with her parents. The male's stated reasons for breaking off the relationship are all attributions. They are *perceived causes of behavior*. But it is interesting to note that the female listening to the male probably is forming attributions about the male's conduct—"Did he really do it for that reason? I think he was more into her than he admits."

Further, both persons in our example are forming impressions of one another. This process of impression formation represents another integral part of attributional phenomena, namely, making *dispositional attributions.* These are inferences about what a person is like. Undoubtedly, the female has formed certain impressions of the male's personality based upon his description of his ill-fated romance. But suppose that in the course of the discussion, she says that she likes to parachute out of airplanes, practice karate, and do pistol target-shooting. It is likely that these comments about her preferred activities will tell the male a lot about the female's dispositions or personality characteristics.

When and why do people make attributions? We know that people do make attributions in various situations. When a perceiver sees a stimulus person take an action, the perceiver may well be concerned with more than simply registering observable events. In our example of the two people who have just met at a party, the female may not be content simply to register the male's stated reasons for why his previous relationship ended. Rather, she may make inferences about the accuracy of the male's stated reasons. Whether he still cares for the other woman, why he might have mentioned the ill fated relationship, whether he has difficulty relating to all women, and whether he would have difficulty relating to her. That is, our female may be motivated to understand, or make dispositional inferences about the underlying nature of the male with whom she is interacting. This need to understand, organize, and form meaningful perspectives about the myriad events people observe every day is considered to be a major goal of attributional processes. Without such an understanding of our social world, events would be unpredictable and uncontrollable.

How do people make attributions that render their experiences understandable, controllable, and predictable? Do they rationally process information and then report reasonable, objective inferences? Do they try to explain events in a light that is more flattering to themselves than would be warranted if a more objective account were rendered? Evidence suggests that each of these processes represents a viable base for attributions. But when one process will be operative and the other relatively inoperative is unclear. Furthermore, there are no doubt mechanisms that govern attributional activity which have not been specified in previous work. Finally, we simply do not know enough about the situations in which people actually engage in attributional activity versus those in which they do not, nor do we know much about different types of attributions (e.g., causal, responsibility, and dispositional attributions) for different situations. Therefore, let the reader beware: the topic of attribution is popular and already has been well-researched, but there are many significant questions remaining to be answered in the future.

In the remainder of this chapter, we will discuss early theoretical works that have formed the foundation for the development of attribution theory and research.

Attributional Aspects of Heider's Common-Sense Psychology

Heider's (1944, 1958) theoretical statements provided the seed for the development of the attribution area in social psychology. Before the publication of Heider's 1958 book *The Psychology of Interpersonal Relations,* there had been few attempts to conceptualize systematically how people perceive and interpret the actions of others. Heider analyzed in detail how people go about answering questions such as: "Did she intend to hurt him by that action?" "What is he really like when you get to know him?" Heider referred to his analysis as "common-sense psychology" or the "naive analysis of action" because he was concerned with the events that occur in everyday life for most people and the manner in which people understand these events and explain them in "common sense" terms. He described his approach in this way: "Our concern will be with 'surface' matters, the events that occur in everyday life on a conscious level, rather than with the unconscious processes studied by psychoanalysis in 'depth' psychology. These intuitively understood and 'obvious' human relations can, as we shall see, be just as challenging and psychologically significant as the deeper and stronger phenomena" (1958, p. 1). We should emphasize, however, that in no sense did Heider's analysis represent a naive conception. Rather, it is an extremely provocative and perceptive theoretical analysis of human social behavior. Researchers have yet to probe adequately many of the eminently researchable ideas contained in Heider's 1958 book.

Heider's Causal Analysis of Perception

At the very heart of Heider's analysis is the view that many principles that underlie person perception have parallels in the field of nonsocial, or object, perception. In *The Psychology of Interpersonal Relations* (1958), Heider presents a comprehensive formulation of the naive, implicit principles that underlie the perception of social objects, "Principles that connect the stimulus configurations presented to a person with his apprehension of them" (p. 21). In other words, his causal description of perception regards the phenomenally given immediate presence of the objects of perception as the end-product of a process. This process may be causally structured into steps.

The initial step in the perception of social objects involves the person toward whom the perceiver's attention is directed. This other person, with his/her psychological processes such as intentions, dispositions, and emotions, is referred to as a *distal stimulus.* Because the distal stimulus is external to and does not directly impact upon the perceiver, information about the distal object (i.e., the person as the object of perception) must be obtained through some form of mediation involving physical stimuli (e.g., light and sound waves). In the case of person perception, the mediation conveys information about the personality of the other as revealed by his/her behavior or from verbal descriptions of the stimulus person's actions made by the third party. The resulting stimulus pattern, or "raw material," with which the perceiver comes into direct contact has been termed the *proximal stimulus*. It is through the mediation that the perceiver and the objects of perception may be said to be causally connected.

The final step in the causal analysis of perception comprises the constructive process within the perceiver which results in the phenomenal percept of the person as experienced by the perceiving organism. In this constructive part of the process, the proximal stimulus may be actively interpreted against a background of subjective forces such as past experiences, wishes, needs, and future expectancies. Percepts will arise that best fit the stimulus conditions and internal systems of evaluations or meanings.

This constructive phase of the perceptual process suggests a hierarchical process, ". . . in which proximal stimulus gives rise to more peripheral meanings, which in turn play the role of data for the higher levels of construction" (Heider, 1958, p. 44). Heider does not, however, argue that this process proceeds in a one-way fashion from proximal stimulus to more central processes (e.g., logical analysis of information, memory processes, belief systems) in the brain. Rather he suggests that there is an interaction between the central processes and the more peripheral stimulus pattern (i.e., the proximal stimulus) such that the former determines in some instances more, in some instances less, how the proximal stimulus is organized and, consequently, how the final percept is phenomenally experienced. That is, in some cases causal information may be inherent in the perceptual organization of information as determined by the properties of the perceptual apparatus (Heider, 1959). In other cases, however, causal information may arise from more deliberative, inferential processes within the perceiver.

According to Heider's analysis of social perception and phenomenal causality, then, attribution processes are inextricably intertwined with perceptual processes and are oriented toward the search for structure or dispositional properties. In this analysis, people are seen as trying to develop organized, meaningful perspectives about the numerous events that they observe everyday for it is only ". . . by referring transient and variable behavior and events to relatively unchanging underlying conditions" (Heider, 1958, p. 79) that individuals can predict and control their environment.

While Heider draws many parallels between the principles underlying social and nonsocial perception, he also admits that there are some differences. He believes, for example, that constancy and invariance (always seeing the person as displaying the same traits) in social perception is not as perfect as it is in nonsocial perception. As an illustration, there is some evidence that a perceiver may tend consistently to attribute a stimulus person's behavior to the person (i.e., to stable personality features of the person) regardless of the situation in which the behavior occurs (see discussion of actor-observer differences, Chapter 2). But Heider's analysis would allow for the possibility that a perceiver *may learn* to view others as responding in differentiated ways in different situations. Thus, the mother may learn to view her son as quiet and obedient at home but difficult to manage at school.

Internal vs. External Attribution

Heider suggests that people search for the causal structure of events via reliance upon attributions to the environment *(external attribution)* or to something in the person involved in the event *(internal attribution)*. Types of external attributions include those made to the physical and social circumstances surrounding the action, while types of internal attributions include those to the actor's ability, motivation, attitude, or emotional state. For example, a teacher may conclude that a student's academic problems in school can be traced to the student's difficult family situation. This conclusion represents an external attribution. On the other hand, an internal attribution would be represented by the teacher's inference that the student's problems could be traced to the student's lack of motivation in studying and working hard to comprehend the subject matter.

Conditions of Action

Heider proposed that an action outcome depends upon a combination of environmental force and personal force. *Environmental force* was conceived to refer to important external factors such as the difficulty of a task. *Personal force* was conceived to involve ability ("can" in Heider's conception) and motivation ("trying"). Heider suggests that people are very sensitive to the extent to which *can* and *trying* are involved in a person's behavior. Heider theorized that the specific components of *can* are ability and power. Trying, according to Heider, has both a directional component (what a person intends to do) and a quantitative component (how hard the person is trying to do something). Heider argued that intention is often taken as the equivalent of wish, or wanting. If, for example, we know that a person is trying to write a book, we usually assume that he or she wants to do it.

In his naive analysis of action, Heider posited that exertion varies directly with the difficulty of the task and inversely with the power or ability of the person. An implication of this point is that the less power or ability individuals have the more they will have to exert themselves to succeed; also, the greatest exertion will be needed when individuals have little power or ability and the task is difficult. This analysis also has implications for the extent to which power or ability will be attributed to a person. For example, great power or ability will be attributed to people if they are able to solve difficult tasks with little exertion. As we can see from this discussion of Heider's naive analysis of action, then, our perception of whether individuals have a particular ability or display motivation in certain situations is important. It may affect our understanding of their actions, our predictions regarding their future behaviors, and our attitudes toward them.

Sometimes it is very clear in the absence or failure of action whether it is the *can* or the *try* that is the missing condition. However, in some circumstances the data are sufficiently ambiguous so that the person's own needs or wishes determine the attribution. As an example of such egocentric attributions, Heider cites the thief who, having no opportunity to steal, considers himself an honest man. In reality, the thief does not steal because the *can* is lacking; he has had no opportunity. However, he attributes his failure to steal to the fact that he has no intention to steal and thus is able to claim credit for being law-abiding. Heider also contends that the actions of others provide a fertile field for egocentric attribution. For example, we may think erroneously that another person is able and intends to do something just because we wish it to happen. Or we may erroneously see ourselves as the focus of other people's actions (i.e., attach too much importance to ourselves in our judgment of how another person sees the world). In general, Heider contends that erroneous judgments are made when the conditions of action are only partially given or when egocentric influences distort the causal inference process. The topic of egocentric aspects of attributional activities constitutes a major strand of research in contemporary attribution work; and we will devote considerable attention to it in subsequent sections of this book.

Concluding Points

Heider's main contribution to attribution theory is his conception of the processes and variables involved in a person's attributions of causality. Heider suggests that people operate very much like quasi-scientists in their attributional activities. They observe an event and then, often in a logical, analytical way, attempt to discover the connections between the various effects and possible causes. Heider does not argue that people are always objective and rational in their attributional behavior. He points out that sometimes people make attributions that are not based on enough information, or an adequate analysis of information, or that are distorted by psychological needs and motivations.

This review of Heider's analyses of social perception and the causal inference process has revealed only a small part of Heider's contribution to contemporary attribution work. His work has been and continues to be a profound stimulus for ideas about attributional behavior.

Jones and Davis' and Jones and McGillis' Theory of Correspondent Inferences

Jones and Davis' (1965) theory of correspondent inferences was the first explicit hypothesis-testing formulation in the area of attribution. This theory set the stage for an upsurge in the amount of research investigating attributional problems. The theory of correspondent inferences is basically concerned with factors that influence an observer's attribution of intent and disposition to another person. It does not explicitly address the question of how individuals understand their *own* intentions and dispositions.

To analyze the process of making correspondent inferences about others Jones and Davis employ attributional principles adopted from Heider. In this formulation, a *correspondent inference* is an inference about individuals' intentions and dispositions that follows directly from or corresponds to their behaviors. If, for example, Jim makes a sarcastic remark to his wife Sally, leading to much emotional distress on the part of Sally, we may infer that Jim is hostile toward Sally and intends to abuse her verbally (our attribution of Jim's intent follows directly from his behavior). We may also make the dispositional inference that Jim is basically a malicious person. Alternatively, we may infer that Jim's sarcastic remark was not intentional and that he means Sally no ill will; to infer malintent here *would not* be a correspondent inference. But how do we decide whether Jim intended to harm Sally and indeed is a rather malicious person? After all, the couple may have had a long history of marital conflict, and the remark may be interpreted mainly in the context of that history of conflict. Jones and Davis have analyzed a number of factors that might help us make this decision.

Desirability of Outcome and Correspondent Inferences

Jones and Davis view the cultural desirability of behavior as an important determinant of the attribution of intent and disposition. According to these theorists, behavior that is unexpected, or low in desirability, will be more informative to the perceiver and more conducive to a correspondent inference than will behavior that is expected, or high in desirability. "Correspondence" in attribution often is operationally defined in terms of how confident the attributor can be in making an inference. In our example of Jim and Sally, we may feel very confident in inferring that Jim is generally rather malicious if his remark is not appropriate for the situation in which it was made. That is, if Jim had made his sarcastic remark to his wife at a cocktail party in front of several of his wife's friends, we likely would feel more confident in our attribution of malintent than if he had been sarcastic during a heated argument that had occurred in his office. In the former situation, Jim's sarcastic behavior toward his wife would be seen as unexpected and socially undesirable and hence would tell us something about Jim's true nature.

A classic study by Jones, Davis, and Gergen (1961) provides evidence about the prediction that behavior which is low in social desirability for a particular role (out-of-role-behavior) will be more informative to a perceiver than will behavior which is high in social desirability (in-role-behavior). In this experiment, subjects heard tape recordings of a person presumably interviewing for a job as a submariner or of a person interviewing for a job as an astronaut. Prior to listening to the taped interview, subjects were given descriptions of the ideal characteristics of candidates for the job. For example, subjects expecting to listen to an interview for the astronaut job were told that the ideal astronaut is a person who is essentially inner-directed (is autonomous, can get along well without interaction with others); subjects expecting to listen to an interview for the submariner job were told that the ideal submariner is a person who is essentially other-directed (gregarious, likes frequent contact with others). In the actual interview, the job candidate, who was thought to understand the requirements for the job, either acted out of line with the requirements for the job (e.g., acted gregarious and other-directed in the case of the astronaut position) or acted in line with these requirements. Subjects were then asked to give their impressions of the person with reference to several traits and how confident they were in their impressions.

Jones et al. found that subjects made more extreme judgments and were more confident about them in the out-of-role condition (where the behavior was unlikely to have been caused by the interview situation) than in the in-role condition (where the behavior could plausibly have been caused by the interview situation). For example, subjects reported that they felt strongly and confidently that the astronaut interviewee was an affiliative, nonindependent type of person when he acted in that manner despite the nonaffiliative, independent nature of the job (in a sense, the out-of-role person was seen as breaking out of the constraints of the situation to show his true self).

Noncommon Effects and Correspondent Inferences

A second important determinant of correspondent inferences is the noncommon effects associated with an action. Noncommon effects represent distinctive outcomes that follow from an act. Only a few studies have been done to investigate this variable (e.g., Newtson, 1974). How the variable works in the attribution process may be shown by an example concerning a person who has chosen an alternative from a set of alternatives.

Let us suppose that we are interested in why Jennifer decided to go to college at Ohio State University rather than the University of Kansas. We may analyze the decisional situation and determine that there are a number of common effects associated with Jennifer's choice. For example, both schools are in the Midwest. Both are state schools. Educational opportunities are about the same at both schools. Both schools are coeducational. Tuition at the two universities is about the same. What about noncommon effects? A major one that may tell us something about Jennifer is that Ohio State University has more than twice the number of students that the University of Kansas has. This one noncommon effect may be very informative in helping us understand Jennifer's choice; in a more confident fashion, we may make an inference about Jennifer's dispositions. We may infer confidently that she is not overly assertive and that she fears large classes where it may be difficult for her to interact with her professors. As this example shows, the fewer the noncommon effects associated with an act, the more likely a correspondent inference will be made. If the choice alternatives differ in countless ways, it will be difficult for the perceiver to infer much about the stimulus person based on the decision made.

Personalism, Hedonic Relevance, and Correspondent Inferences

Correspondence of inferences may also be affected by the perceiver's motivational concerns. The effects of an action are said to have hedonic relevance for the perceiver if the perceiver is benefitted or harmed by the observed action. An act may be hedonically relevant for the perceiver and yet the perceiver may conclude that the consequences of the action were unintended. Alternatively, if the perceiver concludes that the observed action was uniquely conditioned by his or her presence (i.e., that the positive or negative consequences of the action were intended), inferences may be influenced by the variable of personalism. According to Jones and Davis, the more hedonically relevant and/or personalistic an act is for the perceiver, the more likely the perceiver will be to infer that the act reflects a particular intent or disposition. For example, a negative act intentionally directed toward a particular perceiver is more likely to elicit an inference of malevolent intent than the same act directed toward another person.

Despite the potential importance of hedonic relevance and personalism in attributional activities, Jones and Davis paid relatively little attention to the role of motivation in their theory of correspondent inferences. Instead, these theorists focused mainly on the more "rational" aspects of the causal inference process. In the next section, we will review briefly a recent reformulation of Jones and Davis' conception.

Jones and McGillis' (1976) Analysis

Jones and McGillis extended and refined major aspects of Jones and Davis' (1965) formulation. As noted above, Jones and Davis originally proposed that an important determinant of the correspondence of inferences is the extent to which behavioral effects fit the perceiver's prior expectation about what most people desire (i.e., the social desirability of behavioral outcomes). In their analysis, Jones and McGillis suggested that this determinant be refined in such a way that effects are assumed to have valences ranging from −1 to +1. A maximally desirable effect would have a valence of +1, indicating the highest probability that an individual (and most individuals) would want to obtain that effect. Conversely, a maximally undesirable effect would have a valence of −1, indicating the highest probability that an individual (and most individuals) would desire to *avoid* that effect. According to Jones and McGillis, and consistent with Jones and Davis' (1965) earlier formulation of correspondent inference theory, if a particular person pursues an act having a low valence outcome, we should learn more about that person (with a maximum information gain for a −1 outcome) than if the person pursues an act having a high valence. In other words, the more unexpected a given act, the more informative the action is concerning the underlying dispositions of the person.

Jones and McGillis also suggested that the concept of expected valence apply to a second type of expectancy: the perceiver's prior expectations concerning what effect a *particular* actor desires. This latter type of expectancy might be based upon prior knowledge about the actor. A correspondent inference (or information gain) would then constitute a shift in expected valences so that the target person is seen as desiring certain conequences more or less than before the behavioral observation. For example, suppose we observe someone make a series of speeches favoring personal freedom and autonomy, and subsequently observe the same individual make a speech calling for legal prohibitions against the selling and/or use of marijuana. This later speech would disconfirm our prior expectations about this particular actor and would result in more correspondent inferences regarding this actor's beliefs about the deleterious effects of marijuana than if the later speech had merely confirmed the actor's already demonstrated pro-autonomy beliefs.

It is important to note that when the expected valence notion is extended to include expectations based upon an individual's *prior behaviors,* then correspondent inference theory permits analysis of a perceiver's observation over a period of time. This revision of correspondent inference theory by Jones and McGillis (1976) is important because Jones and Davis' (1965) original formulation was concerned only with a single behavioral episode; there was no provision for inferences following more extended experience with a given person. Indeed, Jones and McGillis note that Jones and Davis' ". . . paper might better have been subtitled 'From Acts to Intentions' than 'From Acts to Dispositions.' A disposition is inferred when an intention or related intentions persist or keep reappearing in different contexts" (1976, p. 393). Consequently, the shift from assumed social desirability to assumed valence makes it possible to treat correspondence of inference at any stage in a behavioral sequence.

Another theoretical refinement introduced by Jones and McGillis is the notion of skepticism. As the discrepancy between what the perceiver expects to occur and what actually occurs increases, the perceiver is likely to become skeptical regarding the knowledge gained. For example, Jones, Worchel, Goethals, and Grumet (1971) found that perceivers tended to make rather neutral (i.e., non-correspondent) attributions regarding a black person's attitude when the person did not vote for a candidate favoring affirmative action. In this study, perceivers presumably found the black person's voting record discrepant from what the observer expected and, consequently, viewed with skepticism the information gained about the person's attitude.

Concluding points. Jones and McGillis introduce other new concepts; these concepts relate especially to how perceivers use their unique experiences with particular individuals and their general experiences with categories of persons to infer the attitudes of the stimulus persons. But, in general, Jones and Davis' and Jones and McGillis' correspondent inference theory represents a rational baseline model of the causal inference process. Jones and colleagues present a conception of the perceiver as a rational person who evaluates information and makes logical inferences about others. Jones et al. have focused less on the question of how a perceiver's needs, wishes, and motives influence attributions. However, they have suggested that their theory may serve as a model or norm to identify and study attributional biases. As noted in our discussion of Heider, ego-defensive processes no doubt are at work in attributional phenomena, and increasingly they have become a topic for active research and theoretical analyses. Finally, in these theoretical statements, Jones and colleagues have focused mainly on person perception (or attribution to others) as opposed to self-perception. As we will see below, Kelley, and particularly Bem, have made contributions to understanding self-perception and attribution. Nonetheless, to date, the work by Jones and colleagues represents the most systematic, productive, long-term program of work on processes involved in attribution to others.

Kelley's Contributions to Attribution Theory

Kelley's (1967) review and analysis gave attribution theory and research much stimulation and an integrative approach to understanding both attribution to others and to self. Unlike Jones and colleagues, Kelley assumes that his concepts apply equally as well to self-perception as to person perception.

Analysis of Variance (ANOVA) Model of Attribution

Kelley (1967) theorized that people often make causal attributions as if they were analyzing data patterns by means of an analysis of variance (ANOVA), a statistical technique used to determine whether variance on a dependent variable of interest (that is, the extent to which subjects' scores on a dependent variable differ by condition) exceeds what would be expected by chance. This technique indicates whether an independent variable, such as home background of a student, had a significant effect on a dependent variable, such as performance in the classroom. In terms of attributional processes, the attributor is assumed to attribute effects to those causal factors (the independent variables in this ANOVA analogy) with which they covary, or are correlated with, rather than to those from which they are relatively independent. For example, we might want to know if a student's classroom performance uniquely covaried with home and background factors (and, hence, is attributable to these factors), or if it covaried just as much with other factors such as the learning ability of classmates. The principle of *covariation* between possible causes and effects is the fundamental notion in Kelley's (1967) attributional approach. In Kelley's formulation, the important classes of possible causes are *persons, entities* (things or environmental stimuli), and *times* (occasions or situations).

How can attributors know that attribution of a particular effect to a particular cause is valid? According to Kelley, attributors use three types of information to verify whether they have correctly linked causes and effects. These types of information are the distinctiveness, consistency, and consensus associated with the possible causes. To illustrate the meaning of these types of information, consider an attributor's problem in evaluating why a particular employee in a business frequently was involved in dissension and quarreling with other employees. Kelley's (1967) analysis suggests that the attributor may assess how distinctive the employee's behavior is by asking the question, does the employee quarrel with other people in other situations (e.g., at home or in relating to neighbors)? If so, the behavior is not distinctive and the attribution of causality for the conflict most likely would be directed toward the employee (e.g., his/her unfriendly disposition) as opposed to other people or aspects of the work situation.

How does the attributor use consistency information? If the employee argued and was at odds with others consistently over a period of time and with reference to different issues, then the behavior would be consistent over *time* and *modality,* and again an attribution to the employee's disposition probably would be made. Consensus information would be used to determine whether others also engaged in considerable quarreling at the employee's place of business. If arguing and bickering were commonplace, the attributor might be less likely to attribute the employee's behavior to some personal characteristic. The attributor might guess that conditions at the business were generally unsatisfactory to the employees. On the other hand, if others did not quarrel often, a dispositional attribution would be warranted. In sum, Kelley's (1967) analysis would predict that an attribution to the employee's personal dispositions would be made if the behavior in question was low in distinctiveness, high in consistency, and low in consensus.

Several investigators have reported evidence supporting Kelley's (1967) ideas. In a well-known study, McArthur (1972) examined the causal attributions made by observers of another person's behavior. She presented subjects with person-entity statements (e.g., "Tom is enthralled by the painting.") and three accompanying statements providing information about high or low consensus (high: "Almost everyone who sees the painting is enthralled by it."), distinctiveness (high: "Tom is not enthralled by almost every other painting."), and consistency (high: "In the past, Tom has almost always been enthralled by the same painting."). For each set of information, the subjects were asked to decide what probably caused the event (e.g., Tom to be enthralled by the painting) to occur. Subjects could attribute it to something about the person, something about the entity, something about the particular circumstance, or some combination of two or more of the first three factors. McArthur found that entity attribution (i.e., something about the painting) was relatively frequent when a response was characterized by high consensus, high distinctiveness, and high consistency. She also found that person attribution (i.e., something about Tom) was relatively frequent when a behavior was characterized by low consensus, low distinctiveness, and high consistency. In general, McArthur's results suggest that people can assimilate rather intricate combinations of information and make logical (in the manner suggested by Kelley) inferences based on that information.

Causal Schemata

Kelley (1972a) suggests that while the ANOVA model is appropriate for certain cases when the individual can engage in a relatively complete causal analysis, it is *not* descriptive of most attributional work. According to Kelley, the inferential problem is only infrequently so imposing that it necessitates a full-blown analysis. In many situations, we do not have time to engage in a complete analysis, even if it were advisable. The requirements of modern life frequently lead to hasty deliberations in which decisions are made by reference mainly to present feelings, thoughts, and perceptions, the advice of others, and our past experience. Kelley contends that past experience may provide individuals with a backlog of understanding relative to causal relations and that individuals can call on this store of knowledge when an inference has to be made quickly. This store of knowledge of causal relations represents what Kelley refers to as causal schemata. Kelley says that causal schemata are learned, stored in the person's memory, and then activated by environmental cues. Schemata presumably generalize on the basis of a broad range of objects and situations, and may be stimulated by numerous cues.[1]

Finally, only a few studies have been conducted to test causal schemata ideas (e.g., Cunningham & Kelley, 1975). There are many unanswered questions relating to schemata. For example, how do they develop? Are there pronounced differences among people in their schemata or their use of them? What are the most meaningful schemata, and in what situations are they typically activated?

Discounting

The idea of discounting in attribution was articulated by Kelley in another of his important statements (Kelley, 1972b). This principle relates to the situation involving an attributor who has information about a given effect(s) and a number of possible causes. How are certain causes discounted and others regarded as the real causes? Kelley offers this definition for discounting: "The role of a given cause in producing a given effect is discounted if other plausible causes are also present" (1972b, p. 8). Kelley suggests that discounting is reflected in ways such as a person's feeling of little certainty in the inference that a particular cause led to a particular effect. For example, suppose a male tells a wealthy woman that she is one of the most lovely women in the city; she may feel little certainty about the sincerity of the compliment if she assumes that the male may be trying to get some monetary benefit from interacting with her. (A similar point is made in a study reported by Sigall & Michela, 1976.)

A classic pair of investigations by Thibaut and Riecken (1955) illustrate quite well how the discounting principle works in attributional activity. In one of two parallel studies, an undergraduate male student worked with two other male subjects, who both were actually the experimenter's accomplices. One of the accomplices was revealed to be of higher status (he had just finished his Ph.D. requirements) than the other subject who presumably had just finished his freshman year of college. As the experimental procedure developed, the true subject found it necessary to attempt to influence the two accomplices to help him. Eventually, and at the same time, both agreed to do so. Compliance by the accomplices constituted the effect for which the subject had various plausible causal explanations. He was asked whether each person complied because he wanted to (an internal cause) or because he had been forced to (an external cause). The results showed that subjects attributed the high-status person's compliance to the internal cause and the low-status person's compliance to the external cause.

How does this study illustrate the discounting principle? The possible internal cause of compliance by both the high- and low-status person is the person's own preference, and the external cause is the subject's persuasive power. In the case of the high-status person, the subject's power is not a plausible cause for compliance; therefore, the compliance is attributed to the internal cause. However, the subject's power is a plausible cause for the low-status person's compliance, and given the two plausible causes (including the low-status person's own preference), the role of the internal cause is discounted; thus, the low-status person's behavior is attributed to external pressure.[2]

Augmentation

When there are multiple plausible causes of a given effect and when some of these causes are facilitative and others are inhibitory with respect to the effect, a reverse version of the discounting principle, which has been called the augmentation principle, is necessary. Kelley (1972b) has defined this augmentation principle as follows: "if for a given effect, both a plausible inhibitory cause and a plausible facilitative cause are present, the role of the facilitative cause in producing the effect will be judged greater than if it alone were present as a plausible cause for the effect" (1972b, p. 12). The important idea in this definition is that the facilitative cause must have been extremely potent if the effect occurred despite the opposing effect of the inhibitory cause. For example, if we were to observe an individual perform extremely well on the Graduate Record Examination, despite the fact that this individual was obviously not feeling well, we would likely over-attribute successful performance (in the face of plausible external reasons for unsuccessful performance) to the individual's ability or effort.

Kelley (1972b) reviews a large body of evidence that relates to the discounting and augmentation principles. Nevertheless, it seems likely that these processes will continue to represent a focal topic for future research in attribution theory. Theoretically, there are a number of major questions that remain to be investigated, including: What decisional rules do people use in deciding which of seemingly equivalent causes to discount? Do people often tolerate a number of possible causes without discounting? Do people often discount or augment the importance of plausible causes in line with their self-interests, as opposed to mainly rational considerations?

Concluding Points

In his various writings (especially 1967, 1972a, & b, 1973), Kelley has produced one of the most elegant and elaborate analyses of attributional processes that exist to date. Kelley has made a notable attempt to synthesize person perception (other attribution) and self-perception concepts, and he has developed formal models of how people deliberately analyze information and make inferences and of how they do this very quickly. As was true with the theoretical work of Jones and colleagues, Kelley's analyses have been limited in terms of how powerful motives and emotions interact with logical-rational processes to produce attributional phenomena.

Bem's Contribution to Attribution Theory

In this final section, we will review Daryl Bem's (1967a, 1972) seminal conceptions of how people interpret their own behavior and psychological states. The importance of Bem's contribution to the attribution area first was fully recognized by Kelley (1967) in his perceptive integrative review. Kelley recognized Bem's work on self-perception as a necessary complement to the work by Jones and Davis and others on person perception. Bem (1972) has acknowledged and expanded on the attributional characteristics of his earlier work. This work now has become an important part of the attribution literature, even though it was originally intended to represent an alternative approach to dissonance theory in attitude change research.

Bem (1972) claims that people come to know their own attitudes, emotions, and other internal states partially by inferring them from observations of their own overt behavior and the context in which this behavior occurs. That is, people "look back" and imagine their acts together with the relevant situations in which they occurred, then infer their internal states by means of logical deduction (e.g., "If I was eating scallops, and no one was influencing me to eat them, then I must like scallops."). The strikingly unorthodox implication of Bem's analysis is that people do not know what they think, feel, or believe before they act. It follows, also, that Bem does not consider that attributional change occurs because people do not have priori attributions that exist apart from behavior. Rather Bem asserted that people infer their internal states such as attributions and attitudes after they behave, and cannot remember internal states that are discrepant with their behavior (see Bem & McConnell, 1970). In this conception, people are viewed as strictly information processors, making attributions about themselves based mainly upon observable data. Bem's central proposition is: "Individuals come to 'know' their own attitudes, emotions, and other internal states partially by inferring them from observations of their own overt behavior and/or the circumstances in which this behavior occurs. Thus, to the extent that internal cues are weak, ambiguous, or uninterpretable, the individual is functionally in the same position as an outside observer, an observer who must necessarily rely upon those same external cues to infer the individual's inner states" (1972, p. 2).

Bem traces much of his work to Skinner's (1957) operant behavioristic analysis of human verbal behavior. Bem claims that his theory embodies radical behaviorism because it eschews any reference to internal physiological or conceptual processes. Bem's arguments have engendered considerable debate, especially in the attitude area (e.g., Bem, 1976b; Mills, 1967; Jones, Linder, Kiesler, Zanna, & Brehm, 1968). However, his position has had considerable impact upon contemporary attribution work (e.g., Snyder, 1976). Bem (1972) contended that the 1960s had been dominated by theories concerned with chronic drives toward consistency and uncertainty reduction (e.g., dissonance theory), whereas the 1970s would be dominated by theories emphasizing rational contemplation and information processing. He argued that there was a paradigm shift occurring in social psychology, a shift from motivation/drive models of cognitions to information processing/attribution models—of which self-perception theory was an element. Bem was right in part, and his theoretical work set the pace for this development which will be discussed in greater length in Chapter 2.

Concluding Points

Although Bem (1967, 1972) contended that his work embodied behaviorism, such a contention is not logically supported by the assumption that people *infer* their internal states. Further, Bem's central proposition, as quoted above, is full of theoretical loopholes—"to the extent that internal cues are weak, ambiguous, or uninterpretable. . . ." How do we know whether internal cues should be so characterized in a particular situation? Bem's statements are silent about such reservations as these. Bem's presumably non-motivational perspective also does not address the question of why people make attributions. Indeed, to answer such a question would require invoking some motivational principle, such as a desire to understand or control one's social environment.

These points notwithstanding, Bem's influence has been important. His work has stimulated much research that is clearly attributional in character. Moreover, he was the first theorist concerned with attributional processes to focus exclusively upon self-perception and how people understand their personal states. Finally, Bem focused our attention on behavior to an extent few other contemporary theorists have, and as Bem (1972) remarked, attributional analyses have been especially incomplete in treating the linkages among various types of overt behavior and various classes of cognitions/attributions, and also types of physiological responses.

A Brief Summary and Comparison of Basic Attribution Theories

Before moving on to a discussion of major theoretical advances and extensions, it may be helpful to point out briefly some of the major distinctions between the approaches discussed so far. Heider's naive analysis of action was the germinal work for later theoretical developments; all subsequent analyses contained elements of Heider's formulation. Heider did not provide much empirical foundation for his ideas. Jones and Davis presented the first empirically-grounded attribution statement. These theorists were concerned primarily with person-perception processes, and their analysis focused solely on determinants of attributions to other people. In particular, Jones and Davis were concerned with how perceivers make attributions about the intentions and dispositions of other people. In contrast, Bem's work was concerned solely with the process of self-attribution. He theorized about the process whereby people find out about their own internal states, such as attitudes, beliefs, and emotions. Bem also provided an empirical foundation for much of his theorizing on self-perception processes. Kelley's early work was aimed at synthesizing and integrating work on self and other attributional processes. Recently, empirical investigations of his own particular versions of attribution theory have been actively pursued.

Notes

[1] Although Heider does not label this backlog of past experience as schemata, he too seems to be advancing a notion similar to causal schemata in his assertion that people readily make hundreds of attributions every day.

[2] The astute reader may recognize the similarity between Kelley's discounting principle and Jones and Davis' (1965) noncommon effects-analysis. According to Jones and Davis, correspondence of inferences increases as the number of noncommon effects (in Kelley's terminology, the number of plausible causes) decreases.

Major Theoretical Advances and Extensions

2

In this chapter, we will review major theoretical advances and extensions in the attribution area in the early and mid-1970s. Our treatment will be general and selective. We will describe a continuation of theoretical work from the beginnings by Heider, Jones and colleagues, Kelley, and Bem. But we also will point out how these advances of the 1970s have not led to the type of broad, systematic analyses of attributional phenomena that might have been expected in light of Heider's (1958) magnum opus and the rush of theoretical work in the mid- and late 1970s.

The topics to be covered in this chapter on advances are:

1. Attribution in achievement situations
2. Actor-observer differences in attributed causality
3. Self-esteem processes and self-presentation in attribution activities
4. Lay epistemology
5. Misattribution of arousal
6. A brief commentary on the significance of these advances and extensions

Attribution in Achievement Situations

Weiner and his associates (see Weiner, 1974; Weiner, Russell, and Lerman, 1978) have been leaders in establishing a literature concerning the inference of causality as well as other perceptions and behavior in achievement situations. Weiner (1974) has argued that his findings—deriving mainly from subjects' reading and reacting to hypothetical situations presented by the investigator—can be generalized to real world contexts in which teachers make inferences about students, and reward and punish them for performances differing along certain dimensions. Weiner et al.'s focus on the "can" and "trying" components of perceived causality phenomena reveal the strong impact of Heider's writings on their work.

In early work, Weiner and colleagues (1972) hypothesized that people infer causality about stimulus persons' success or failure on the basis of perceptions about the persons' ability on the task in question, how much effort was expended, how difficult the task was, and how much luck influenced the outcome. Ability and effort were considered to be properties internal to the persons, while task difficulty and luck were considered to be external to the persons. Also, ability and task difficulty were treated as stable determinants; whereas, effort and luck were treated as unstable determinants. The antecedents of these determinants of achievement-related attributions were theorized to be factors such as social norms, past success history, causal schemata, and certain individual differences such as sex.

In the area of individual differences, Weiner and his associates have produced substantial evidence showing that individuals classified as high or low in need for achievement have disparate attributional biases. Weiner et al. (1972) reported that high need achievers typically attribute success to high ability and effort (properties of the self) and failure to lack of effort. Such tendencies have been found to be associated with heightened reward of self or rating of pride in accomplishment on the part of persons high in need achievement. However, persons low in need achievement most frequently attribute failure to low ability; further, they usually exhibit no clear attributional preference in light of successful performance. This latter effect is associated with relatively moderate reward of self or rating of pride in accomplishment by low need achievers.

Research by Frieze and Weiner (1971) provides an example of early work on the theoretical ideas advanced by Weiner and his associates. These investigators employed Kelley's principles concerning covariation information used in making attributions to examine achievement judgments. The procedure involved giving subjects information that specified the percentage of success a hypothetical person experienced at a task (100%, 50%, or 0%). The subjects also were provided information (i.e., descriptions of hypothetical situations) about the degree of prior success or failure at a task (the distinctiveness of the outcome), the degree of success or failure at similar tasks (the consistency of the behavior), and the performance of others at the task (consensus). The subjects then attributed the immediate success or failure of the stimulus person to ability, effort, task difficulty, and luck. The data revealed these main patterns: (1) Outcomes for which there was high consensus in performance were ascribed to characteristics of the task. (2) Success was attributed to internal factors, while failure was attributed to external factors. (3) Behavior inconsistent with past performance was attributed to the unstable variables of luck and effort. (4) The greater the degree of prior success or failure, the greater was the tendency for respective success and failure to be attributed to high or low ability. Based on these findings, Frieze and Weiner concluded that people are able to form systematic causal judgments in complex achievement situations.

Extensions of Earlier Conception

Weiner and associates have extended their conception as described in early writings. They now have considered other causes of success and failure (e.g., mood, fatigue), another causal dimension (intentionality), causal effects such as expectancy shifts and affective reaction, and certain behavioral consequences (e.g., persistence at a task, response rate). Table 2.1 provides a partial description of the current model.

The introduction of intentionality into the model has created a problem; the dimensions of causality no longer appear orthogonal. Weiner, Russell, and Lerman (1978) indicate that intentionality implies volitional control which implies instability. However, a person could be perceived to be an intentionally and stably patient individual. Weiner et al. have conducted little, if any, research directly concerned with the intentionality cause. They do suggest that its introduction indicates a caution that the placement of a cause within a dimension (e.g., ability in the stable dimension) *need not be invariant over time or between people.*

The import of such qualification about causes and dimensions is reinforced in research by Ostrove (1978), who suggests that on occasion effort may operate as if it were a stable factor, even as it often appears to be a transient factor. Ostrove notes that the perception of effort as stable is illustrated by people's image of a person as a hardworker—with "nose to the grindstone." To some extent, the "hard-worker" image corresponds to what Weiner and associates (e.g., Rest, Nierenberg, Weiner, & Heckhausen, 1973) have called effort as a trait, as opposed to effort as a state (that is variable).

Weiner et al. have directed more attention toward investigating what they call causal effects than toward probing behavioral consequences. They argue that ascriptions for success and failure in part determine the direction and magnitude of expectancy shifts. For example, failure that is attributed to low ability should decrease the expectation of future success more than failure imputed to bad luck or fatigue.

Weiner and associates have argued and produced data showing that reports of pride and shame are maximized when achievement outcomes are attributed internally, and minimized when achievement outcomes are imputed externally. For example, success attributed to high ability or hard work is expected to produce more pride than success ascribed to good luck. Success ascribed to good luck is expected to lead to a lesser increment in the subjective expectancy of future success, hence less pride, than success ascribed to high ability.

Attribution Retraining

An important study conducted by Dweck (1975) employed reasoning derived from Weiner et al.'s conception to retrain children who were unsuccessful in school work and who de-emphasized effort as a determinant of their performance. All children-subjects met stringent criteria for having little feeling of control over their school performance and little success in a school situation. In Dweck's training situation, the children were given one of two different treatment procedures over a period of twenty-five days. One-half of the children received only success experiences (e.g., easy problems to solve accompanied by success feedback). The other half of the children received what Dweck called attribution retraining. Although here too success predominated, several failure trails were programmed each day. On the occasions when failure occurred, the failure was

Table 2.1

Weiner et al.'s Current Attributional Model of Achievement Motivation (Adapted from Weiner, Russell, and Lerman, 1978)

Theorized Causal Direction	Causes of Success and Failure	→ Causal Dimensions	→ Causal Effects
	Ability		
	Effort	Stability ———————► Expectancy Shifts (stable, unstable)	
	Task difficulty		
	Luck	Locus of Control ——► Affective reaction (internal, external) (e.g., pride or shame)	
	Mood		
	Fatigue		
	Teacher bias	Intentionality	
	Others		

attributed by the experimenter to a lack of effort. Thus, these subjects received direct instruction in how to interpret the causes of their failures.

Dweck found that when children in the two groups were taken back to the original situation and re-tested, attribution retraining subjects showed improvement in their emphasis upon effort to overcome failure when it occurred, and they ultimately showed much improvement in actual performance. Subjects in this group who sometimes failed were overheard to say such things as "I missed that one. That means I have to try harder." On the other hand, subjects in the success-only group showed little improvement in performance, nor much change in their emphasis upon effort to overcome failure.

Dweck and Goetz (1978) suggest that "attribution may be enmeshed in the complex psychological dynamics of an individual's sometimes desperate attempts to understand and thereby more adequately cope with trying personal problems" (p. 155). The implication of this type of work for practical educational activities with children was presaged by Weiner (1973), who called for and pointed out the benefits of early education programs which teach affective-motivational development, rather than intellectual functioning. We should emphasize, however,

**→ Behavioral
Consequences**

Intensity

Choice

⟶ Persistence

Response rate

Resistance to extinction

Time to problem solution

that there no doubt are limitations to the attribution retraining procedure for implementation in real educational settings. For example, there may be situations in which attribution to ability is warranted when failure occurs. A child may be limited in quantitative skill; and to retrain the child to attribute failure on quantitative tasks to lack of effort may result in considerable frustration as well as little improvement in skill.

Concluding Points on Weiner et al.'s Conception

Weiner et al. have made several important contributions to understanding attributional phenomena. However, the limitations of the work must be noted. Almost all of the research by Weiner et al. has been conducted using hypothetical situations in which subjects reveal their perceptions or feelings in a fashion presumably that would hold if they were more involved in the events as witnesses or participants. This simulational procedure may be quite limited in the generalized applicability of the results deriving from it to real world events and settings. The critic may ask whether subjects in these designs are analyzing the information presented to them in a way that would parallel their analysis in settings where such analysis was more meaningful (e.g., in actual school settings or in close interpersonal relations). Or are the subjects experiencing the same type or level of affect that they would in more natural settings?

A related criticism is that Weiner and colleagues have provided little process or manipulation check evidence (e.g., that subjects indeed do perceive ability to be an invariant state). These investigators emphasize the subjective side of causality; yet they have not typically provided data on a range of theoretically meaningful perceptions and emotions. While their theoretical work is elaborate, the supportive empirical work is lacking at certain major points.

On the positive side, there is much to be said about the contributions of Weiner et al. They have examined, as have no other investigators, the role of affect in attributional phenomena. The same point holds for their extensive probing of individual differences variables, especially need for achievement. Weiner et al. have developed a program of work on achievement-related attributions that has substantial implication for educational practice and philosophy (as revealed, for example, by Dweck's work). Finally, Weiner and associates have provided by far the most sophisticated extension of Heider's concepts of *can* and *trying,* and they have shown the import of these concepts for perceived causality and behavior.

Actor-Observer Differences in Attributed Causality

Jones and Nisbett's (1972) Divergent Perspectives Hypothesis

One of the provocative extensions of basic attribution ideas has been concerned with the question of how people with different perspectives diverge in their attributions about the causes of the same behavior. This concern with divergence in attribution emanates mainly from Jones and Nisbett's (1972) influential theoretical statement on actor-observer differences in the attribution of causality. Jones and Nisbett's analysis was influenced in part by the following ideas presented by Heider (1958): "It seems that behavior in particular has such salient properties it tends to engulf the total field rather than be confined to its proper position as local stimulus whose interpretation requires the additional data of a surrounding field—the situation in social perception" (p. 54). "The person tends to attribute his own reactions to the object world, and those of another, when they differ from his own to personal characteristics in O [other]" (p. 157).

In their statement, Jones and Nisbett hypothesize that actors will attribute causality or responsibility for their behavior to situational influences, whereas observers will attribute causality for the same behavior to stable dispositions possessed by the actors. Jones and Nisbett argue that actors and observers frequently possess different background data for evaluating the significance of an action. Actors generally know more about their behavior and present experiences than do observers. Jones and Nisbett suggest that this background knowledge may divert actors from making a dispositional attribution; that is, actors' attributions may be influenced by their recollection that their behavior has shown variance in similar situations in the past. Observers probably lack information about the distinctiveness and consistency of the actors' behavior. Because of this deficiency in background data, observers may tend to focus their causal analysis on actors and their presumed stable personality dispositions.

As an example of how this actor-observer bias might operate in a natural setting, consider a situation in which a medium-sized city is in great financial distress for many years; but then after a new city manager takes office, the city's situation improves to the point of much economic prosperity and promise. The city's residents not having a full understanding of the influences on the city's economy may attribute the prosperity to the new manager's ability. The city manager, however, may attribute the emerging prosperity to the correction of past mismanagement of city funds, help from the federal government, and a new tax on items commonly bought by tourists visiting the city—all external situational-circumstantial factors.

Jones and Nisbett also contend that different aspects of the available information are salient for actors and observers, and that this differential salience affects the course and outcome of the attribution process. Because actors' sensory receptors are poorly located for observing themselves in action, they may tend to direct their attention to the situational cues with which their behavior is coordinated. To actors, these salient aspects of the environment are the determinants of their behavior. From the observer's perspective, these situational cues may be obscured by the actors' behavior (Heider's "behavior engulfs the field" idea; see also Taylor & Fiske, 1978). The observer, therefore, may tend to assign major responsibility for the actors' behavior to dispositional qualities possessed by the actors.

Evidence about Actor-Observer Attributional Difference

Nisbett, Caputo, Legant, and Marecek (1973) and Storms (1973) provided early evidence relevant to Jones and Nisbett's divergent perspectives hypothesis. Nisbett and associates created one experimental situation in which observers watched actors either comlpy or not comply with an experimenter's request that they volunteer their time in service on a particular project for their university. As the investigators had predicted, observers tended to assume that actors would behave in the future in ways similar to those they had just witnessed, whereas actors made no inferences about their own future behavior. In other words, observers saw actors as very fixed and static in their behavior, but actors did not have the same image of themselves. Actors perhaps thought that their future behavior would depend on the circumstances then prevailing. In a second study by Nisbett et al., indirect support for the divergent perspectives hypothesis was revealed in the finding that college students described their best friends' choice of girl friends and college majors by reference to dispositional qualities of their best friends but that they described their own similar choice in terms of properties of the girl friends or majors.

Storms (1973) provided more direct evidence that an observer attributes an actor's behavior to his or her disposition, whereas the actor attributes the same behavior to the situation. Storms used videotape to provide the actors with a repeated view of their original visual orientations or with a new view of the observer's visual orientation of the actors' behavior (a simple discussion between two people); the observers received either a repeated view of actors or a new visual orientation of how actors saw the situation. Importantly, Storms showed that the actor-observer tendency hypothesized by Jones and Nisbett can be observed if actors and observers maintain their usual visual perspective but that, with a reversal of perspective, the tendency can be reversed, the observer now making more situational attributions than the actor. Storms' study provides evidence in support of Jones and Nisbett's (1972) argument that actor-observer divergencies are due in part to differential foci of attention; his results suggest that when the foci are reversed, the attributional divergencies may be reversed too.

Some Qualifying Evidence

Harvey, Arkin, Gleason, and Johnston (1974) and Harvey, Harris, and Barnes (1975) have found that observers are sensitive to the conditions surrounding an actor's behavior and do not simply make attributions to the actor without consideration of those conditions. Jones and Nisbett's (1971) statement does not include how contextual conditions might affect an observer's attributions to an actor. In the study by Harvey et al. (1974), actors took actions that were expected to have and actually did have either a positive or a negative outcome. When the effect was *discrepant* with the expectation (for example, when a positive outcome had been expected, but a negative outcome occurred), observers who were in the same situation attributed much more causality to the actor than when the effect was not discrepant. Harvey and associates argued that a discrepancy between expected and actual events makes the actor's behavior highly salient and hence draws observers' attributions to him or her.

In the study by Harvey et al. (1975), actors took actions that had either a moderately negative or a strongly negative effect on another person. The results showed that the actors attributed less responsibility to themselves the more negative the effect on the other person. The authors argued that these results reflected actors' need to maintain self-esteem in light of a potentially culpable personal act. It also was found that the more negative the effect the more responsibility the observers attributed to the actor. Presumably, according to Harvey et al. (1975), observers feel a greater need to control the actor's behavior the more negative it is, and they use their attributions toward attainment of this goal.

A Methodological Note

Since the publication of Jones and Nisbett's (1972) statement, considerable work has been directed toward examining conditions under which qualifications of the divergent perspectives tendency will obtain. Much of this work is reviewed by Zuckerman (1979). A conclusion emerging from this review is that while many qualifying conditions have been specified, comparison of the results of studies is difficult because of the diversity of procedures used. For example, in some studies, subjects play the role of actors or observers in hypothetical situations, whereas, in other studies, actors and observers are present in either interpersonal influence or achievement-performance situations. Significantly, it may be concluded from Zuckerman's review that quite different results may be expected for the same variables in these different research settings. The import of this conclusion is revealed most clearly by consideration of the paradigm in which people are asked to imagine being actors or observers in a hypothetical situation. These subjects are not apt to experience the level of involvement felt by actual actors and observers. Consequently, their attributional tendencies may be relatively tempered. Hypothetical actors may experience little of the motivational tension that may occur often when success or failure or positive or negative outcomes are associated with behavior. Furthermore, hypothetical observers do not have the literal focus on an actor and the actor's behavior—a focus which may intensify dispositional attributional tendencies. Logically, there are so many differences between hypothetical and participant situations that it is virtually impossible to assess clearly the comparability of operations and data.

Although the hypothetical situation format was useful in early work in various areas of attribution research, it seems clear that future work will have a stronger potential for ecological generalizability to the extent that more involving situations are sampled. Also, a concerted focus on such situations may lead to more coherence in findings and qualifying conclusions relevant to the divergent perspectives hypothesis.

Reformulation

In a recent step toward reformulating the divergent perspectives hypothesis, Monson and Snyder (1977) reviewed data relevant to this hypothesis and develop a number of qualifying propositions. Based upon their assessment of the evidence, Monson and Snyder suggested that when a behavior has been performed in a situation *chosen* by the actor, actors will make more dispositional attributions than will observers. However, they also suggested that for behaviors performed in situations not chosen by the actor, actors will make more situational attributions than will observers. Monson and Snyder further contended that whether actors or observers, individuals may differ in a *general way* in their inclinations to make situational or dispositional inferences; some may be more inclined to be internal or external in a relatively pervasive way (e.g., Rotter, 1966; de Charms,

1968). Monson and Snyder proposed that an actor's intentionality is a critical determinant of actor-observer differences. They contended that when an act leads to an outcome that is *not intended,* the attributions of actors ought to be more situational than those of observers. What about variables that specifically influence the observer? Monson and Snyder reviewed data showing that when observers are led to empathize with the actors' position, observers should be no more likely to make dispositional attributions than actors (Regan & Totten, 1975). This empathy set variable is similar in its effect to the perspective alteration variable examined by Storms (1973).

A study by Gould and Sigall (1977) provides further evidence about the role of empathy in influencing an observer's attributional perspective to become the functional equivalent of an actor's perspective. These investigators gave observers a set to empathize with a target person (e.g., observers were told "While you are watching him, picture to yourself just how he feels. . . . Try to forget yourself."), or simply to observe the person. Subsequently, observers watched a videotape of a target male attempting to make a good first impression on a female. They then learned that the target person had either succeeded or failed at making a good first impression and were asked to make attributions for his outcome. As Gould and Sigall had predicted, observers given empathic instructions attributed the target person's success to dispositional causes and his failure to situational causes. That is, they exhibited a pattern generally similar to that shown by actors in research such as that by Harvey et al. (1974). Gould and Sigall's study provides further evidence about the importance of the interaction of the attributor's perspective (or cognitive set toward the event persons involved in it) and the nature or valence (e.g., positive or negative outcome) of the event in affecting how actors and observers will diverge or converge in their causal attributions.

Concluding Points about Actor-Observer Differences

Monson and Snyder concluded their analysis with the very reasonable suggestion that researchers turn from attempts to verify the divergent perspectives hypothesis to systematic investigations of the *when, why,* and *with what implications* for attribution theory of differences between actors and observers. Divergence in attribution would seem to represent an area that has major significance in many practical relationships (e.g., manager and worker, husband and wife, parent and child) and should continue to be a major area for attribution research in coming years. Extensive knowledge of divergence is far from complete. For example, we know that people often take account of the persons with whom they will communicate their attributions and that this factor may influence actor-observer differences (see Wells, Petty, Harkins, Kagehiro, & Harvey, 1977). However, we know little about the effects of different types of perceived social audiences on actor-observer differences. As observed by Bem (1972), the full exploration of the rich and intriguing implications of Jones and Nisbett's divergent perspectives hypothesis will probably constitute a major direction in research on attributional processes for many years.

Self-esteem Processes and Self-presentation in Attributional Activities

The investigation of attributional biases, such as the actor-observer differences proposed by Jones and Nisbett (1972), is of importance primarily because it may help us to elucidate basic attributional processes. Attribution theorists historically have been concerned with cognitive processes involved in self and interpersonal perception, and perhaps for this reason, most writers interested in attributional activities have stressed the importance of informational as opposed to motivational sources of bias (e.g., Bem, 1972; Jones & Nisbett, 1972; Kelley, 1967). This information-processing approach to understanding attributional biases has aroused considerable sympathy. Indeed, Lee Ross (1979) has advocated that we *abandon* motivational concerns and concentrate on informational, perceptual, and cognitive factors that may account for systematic biases in attributions of causality. Other writers, however, have urged a more balanced approach in investigating potential mediating causes of attributional biases, noting that the most reasonable theory of the causal inference process likely will involve a precise articulation of the interaction of motivation and cognition (e.g., Shaver, 1975; Weary Bradley, 1978; Weary, 1980). In his seminal analyses of person perception and attribution processes, Heider also noted the necessity of considering the interdependence of motivation and cognition in attributional processes:

Since one's idea includes what "ought to be" and "what one would like to be" as well as "what is," attributions and cognitions are influenced by the mere subjective forces of needs and wishes as well as by the more objective evidence presented in the raw material (Heider, 1958, pp. 120–121).

Much of the controversy surrounding the existence of cognitive versus motivational distortions in attributions of causality has focused on empirical evidence relevant to individuals' self-attributions of causal responsibility for outcomes attendant to their behaviors. A substantial body of literature has demonstrated a tendency for individuals to make greater self-attributions for their own positive behaviors than for their own negative behaviors (see review by Weary Bradley, 1978). The operation of self-serving, or ego-defensive biases has generally been used to explain these results. By taking credit for good acts and denying blame for bad outcomes, an individual presumably may be able to enhance or protect his or her self-esteem.

Miller and Ross (1975) have questioned this self-serving bias interpretation of positive-negative outcome differences in self-attributions. These authors have contended that the results of many of the studies often cited as support for self-serving attributional biases could readily be "interpreted in information-processing terms" (p. 224). Specifically, they have contended that the observed tendency for individuals to accept greater responsibility for positive than for negative outcomes may occur for any or all of several reasons: (a) individuals intend and expect success more than failure and are more likely to make self-ascriptions for expected than unexpected outcomes; (b) perceived covariation between response and outcome may be more apparent for individuals experiencing a pattern of increasing success than for individuals experiencing constant failure; and (c) people erroneously base their judgments of the contingency between response and outcome in terms of the occurrence of the desired outcome (i.e., success) rather than any actual degree of contingency.

While the results of early studies supposedly demonstrating self-serving biases may be subject to alternative, nonmotivational interpretations such as those presented by Miller and Ross (1975), Weary Bradley (1978) argued in a recent review that newer, methodologically improved research provides more conclusive evidence in support of the existence of motivational distortions in the causal inference process. In this paper, Weary Bradley (1978) also presented a broadened formulation to account for seemingly counterdefensive attributions (i.e., attributions indicating greater acceptance of responsibility by the attributor for negative than for positive outcomes attendant to his or her behavior). Specifically, this author suggested that self-serving attributions may be viewed as public self-presentations designed to maximize public esteem needs (though private esteem needs certainly may be implicated), and that in certain conditions, such esteem needs may be best served by accepting responsibility for negative outcomes. That is, individuals might not want to accept undue credit for positive outcomes and deny credit for negative outcomes if they are explicitly told that their performances are the major object of study and if their unrealistically positive self-presentations could be invalidated by their own subsequent behaviors or by others' present/future assessments of their behaviors. The embarrassment resulting from such public invalidation would likely threaten individuals' positive public images.

What Constitutes a Self-Serving Attribution

In an attempt to define what constitutes a self-serving attribution, Miller (1978) suggested that attributions for positive and negative outcomes can represent either distortions in perception of causality or distortions in descriptions of causality (c.f. Weary Bradley, 1978). That is, ". . . they can serve to protect or enhance how the person perceives him/herself" or ". . . they can serve to protect or enhance how *others* perceive the person" (Miller, 1978, p. 1221).

The major issue underlying Miller's differentiation of two types of self-serving attributions involves the *locus* of distortion in the causal inference process (i.e., a perceptual versus a response bias). However, as Weary (1979) recently has noted, there probably are multiple points of bias in the attribution process, from input to output, and present evidence does not allow us to determine the precise point at which bias or defensiveness may be occurring. At this point in time, then, ". . . a more pertinent empirical question would seem to be how and under what conditions self-serving motivations influence attributions of causality" (Weary, 1979, p. 1419).

Lay Epistemology

In this section, we will briefly discuss recent theoretical work by Kruglanski and his colleagues on what they refer to as lay epistemology. Kruglanski, Hamel, Maides, and Schwartz (1978) provided this general description of their focus: "The content of naive epistemology is the laymen's total set of concepts pertaining to the world of experience. The epistemic logic is the assessment criterion, the fulfillment of which yields a sense of valid knowledge. The course of lay inquiry is the sequency of cognitive operations intended to assess the possibility of significant new knowledge" (p. 302).

Kruglanski and associates claimed that their approach subsumes previous formal models (e.g., Kelley's 1967 model) concerning how people deliberately analyze situations and make causal inferences. These theorists argued that the layperson essentially uses one type of logic in validating attributions, namely: The person considers a hypothesis such as "Is it a table" by evaluating the consistency of the implications of the hypothesis—"it is flat," "it has legs," "people eat on it." If they are consistent, the hypothesis is confirmed. Kruglanski et al. did not tell us how much consistency is necessary for the layperson to conclude that a hypothesis is confirmed. But they said that all other attributional validational criteria (e.g., consensus and distinctiveness) are subsumed by this principle. Kruglanski et al. theorized that in applying this principle, the layperson in many situations formulates questions and conjectual answers and then evaluates them against the evidence.

The evidence Kruglanski et al. advanced to support their position is indirect and does not show that people necessarily *feel* that certain pieces of knowledge are consistent and others inconsistent. For example, they showed that people may have a relatively great preference for information that is highly relevant to an event (e.g., "John laughed at the comedian"); highly relevant information might include a means-ends datum such as "The comedian is John's supervisor." The preference for this type of information is relative to general information believed to be important in other models (e.g., consensus, "others did not laugh at the comedian").

These results help to illustrate the Kruglanski et al. position, but they do not show that people use only consistent criteria in making attributions. People cannot always calculate which information is consistent or highly relevant to an attribution. Also, as implied above, in many situations there are mixes of data both consistent and inconsistent with early hypotheses we form. In these situations, the criteria described by theorists such as Heider, Kelley, and Jones are quite essential to the layperson. If I have a mixture of personal information about my hypothesis that "She loves me," then it is very likely I will use consensus information and evaluate whether or not important others think she loves me too.

Endogenous-Exogenous Distinction

An early paper by Kruglanski (1975) provided part of the seed for the Kruglanski et al. analysis. This paper described a partition in attributions between those *endogenous*, where an action is attributed to itself as a reason (an end in itself), and those *exogenous*, where an action is not an end itself but rather is a means to an end. Kruglanski (1975) presented this distinction as a replacement for the internal-external partition that has been used so extensively in attribution research. However, aside from a modicum of empirical work—much of which was carried out by Kruglanski and colleagues—little systematic attention has been given to the endogenous-exogenous distinction among attribution investigators (see Kruglanski, 1977). The internal-external dichotomy continues to be pervasive in extant work, perhaps because of its intuitive appeal and appearance as a contruct in everyday language and thinking.

Misattribution of Arousal

The one other extension of early theorizing to be described in this chapter concerns Zillmann's (1978) three-factor model of attribution of emotion. This model will be reviewed not because of its centrality as an attribution conception, but because of its extension of a very influential early work by Schachter and Singer (1962) concerned wih determinants of the emotion (see also chapter 7 for discussion of Schachter and Singer's work). Schachter and Singer's work deserves major attention because of its influence on attribution research. It has inspired theoretical and empirical work, controversy, and alternative models, such as Zillman's conception. See Valins and Nisbett (1972) for further discussion of the stimulus value of Schachter and Singer's approach in attributional analysis.

Schachter and Singer's Work

Schachter and Singer (1962) proposed that cognitive factors and physiological arousal interact to produce emotion. They presented three main hypotheses:

1. Given a state of physiological arousal for which an individual has no immediate explanation, the individual will label this state and describe personal feelings in terms of available cognitions.
2. Given a state of physiological arousal for which an individual has a completely appropriate explanation, no evaluative needs will arise, and the individual is unlikely to label personal feelings in terms of available cognitions.
3. Given the same cognitive circumstances, the individual will react or describe personal feelings as emotions only to the extent that the individual experiences a state of physiological arousal.

Schachter and Singer's theoretical position is referred to as a two-factor model because of its emphasis upon physiological arousal and interpretation. In this account, heightened, diffuse arousal requires an explanation through some form of cognitive appraisal of the immediate situation. Although Schachter and Singer did not describe their model as an attributional conception, subsequent theorists have viewed it as in large part such a conception (see London & Nisbett, 1974).

In a classic investigation designed to test this model, Schachter and Singer (1962) gave some subjects epinephrine, an activating agent, and no information about the arousing effects of the agent. Another group of subjects was given epinephrine and valid information about its effects, while others were given misinformation or not informed about its effect. A final group (non-aroused) was given a saline injection and was not told what to expect from the injection. After the injection, subjects were exposed to an experimental accomplice who was acting in an angry or euphoric manner. The extent to which subjects imitated the accomplice was recorded, as were subjects' ratings of their emotions.

Table 2.2 presents means for emotional behavior for the conditions described above.

As expected, subjects in the epinephrine-ignorant and epinephrine-misinformed groups imitated the accomplice more than did subjects in the epinephrine-informed condition; also, these subjects rated their emotions as consistent with the accomplice's apparent emotional states. Presumably, subjects in the former conditions were aroused, had no appropriate explanation for their arousal, observed the accomplice's emotional behavior, and concluded that this emotion applied to them too. Subsequent work (e.g., Valins, 1966) has shown that individuals' mere belief that they are aroused is sufficient along with contextual information (e.g., observing the accomplice's emotional behavior) to lead to an attribution of emotion.

Maslach's and Marshall and Zimbardo's Critiques

Recently, the work of Schachter and Singer (1962) has been called into question by Maslach (1979) and Marshall and Zimbardo (1979). Maslach suggested that Schachter and Singer's position is weak because people's search for a cognitive explanation of an arousal state is more extensive than Schachter and Singer assumed and biased toward negative emotional labels. She further argued that the drug injection procedure used by Schachter and Singer was flawed because of imprecise control of timing and magnitude of arousal. In a modified replication of their procedure, using hypnosis instead of drug injection, Maslach manipulated whether or not subjects experienced unexplained arousal in the presence of an experimental accomplice who was displaying either happy or angry emotions. Maslach also carried out an exact replication of Schachter and Singer's procedure. She found that subjects with unexplained arousal reported negative emotions regardless of the accomplice's mood. Maslach concluded that a lack of explanation about arousal biases a person's search toward negative emotion. She emphasized that this conclusion differs from Schachter and Singer's view that the lack of explanation leads to an unbiased search. A final finding of note was that subjects' behavior was sociable when the accomplice acted happy.

Table 2.2

Effects of Physiological Arousal and Information about Arousal on Emotional Behavior (Adapted from Schachter and Singer, 1962)

State of Arousal	Accomplice's Behavior	
	Euphoric	Angry
Nonaroused (saline-injected)	16.0	.8
Physiologically Aroused (epinephrine-injected)		
Informed	12.7	−.2
Ignorant	18.3	2.3
Misinformed	22.6	− −

Note: The higher the score, the more euphoria or anger the subjects displayed. An epinephrine-injected, misinformed condition was not run with the angry accomplice.

Since subjects' reported emotions were negative, Maslach argued that this sociable behavior was "managed" so as to be socially acceptable in that setting.

Marshall and Zimbardo (1979) replicated and extended Schachter and Singer's procedure. Like Maslach, they too found that unexplained arousal produced negatively-toned reports of affect. Further, negative affect was produced merely by the expectation of epinephrine side effects. Unlike Schachter and Singer, Marshall and Zimbardo found no evidence that subjects with inadequately explained epinephrine-produced arousal were more susceptible than placebo controls to the induction of affect by exposure to an accomplice who modeled euphoric behavior. Contrary to Schachter and Singer, Marshall and Zimbardo concluded that there is a lack of "emotional plasticity" in the procedure involving unexplained epinephrine-produced arousal. They also concluded that this type of arousal is associated with negative affect. Overall, Maslach and Marshall and Zimbardo argued that awareness of one's strong arousal without adequate explanations is most likely to be interpreted as a negative mood state.

This discussion would not be complete without brief consideration of Schachter and Singer's (1979) commentary on these critiques. They concluded that pronounced differences in Maslach's procedure (especially regarding timing of emotional experience and when information is given regarding the emotion to be expected) render her work and data noncomparable to their own. As for the Marshall and Zimbardo work, Schachter and Singer also argued that there were such substantial differences in the two studies that no clear comparative conclusions can be drawn. Overall, they claimed that their critics have overlooked a large body of work that reveals considerable emotional "plasticity" associated with unexplained arousal. Interestingly, Schachter and Singer also concluded that given contemporary ethical guidelines for human research, it is unlikely that ever again will anyone do experiments such as theirs and those by Maslach and Marshall and Zimbardo. In essence, they are suggesting that the plasticity issue in this research paradigm may forever remain inconclusive.

Zillmann's Analysis

Zillmann (1978) pointed out that according to Schachter and Singer's conception, an emotion cannot be experienced until an excitatory state materializes, is recognized, and is labeled. Zillmann contended that this conception failed to explain why the individual responds in an aroused fashion to certain stimulus conditions in the first place. Rather, as Zillmann argued, the Schachter-Singer approach simply presupposes that cognitive or situational factors trigger physiological processes, and it then deals with what happens after the individual becomes aware of these processes. Zillmann, thus, concluded that this approach is incomplete because it does not address the very origin of an emotional reaction He suggested that Schachter and Singer had developed a theory that applies only to the emotional experience of people who have developed the skills necessary to engage in full-fledged attributional search activities.

Zillmann's (1978) own approach was designed to eliminate the shortcomings of the Schachter-Singer approach. Zillmann introduced a three component model that emphasizes: (1) a *dispositional* component responsible for immediate, motoric emotional reaction (e.g., shaking or blushing), without interpretive activity; (2) an *excitatory* component that energizes behavior because of unconditioned or learned habits (this is the heightened arousal state of the organism); and (3) an *experiential* component which involves the conscious experience of either the motor or the excitatory reaction or of both; it involves an appraisal or attributional element.

Zillmann indicated that after the dispositional motoric response, the excitatory reaction can be seen as preparing the individual to act on the situation so as to avert a potential threat. No attributional search by the individual is conceived to be necessary to find an appropriate explanation for this reaction. Search behavior is seen to be forced upon the individual, especially in ambiguous response situations. In such situations, both dispositional and excitatory reactions are posited to be mediated by the attributional element of the experiential component of emotion.

Zillmann reviewed diverse evidence, including work on aggression (e.g., Zillmann & Cantor, 1976) and sexual excitement (e.g., Cantor, Zillman, & Bryant, 1975) as supportive of the three-factor model. In general, Zillmann argued that people in emotional situations often do make attributions but that they may do so in a sporadic, noncontinuous way. He implied that people may "overreact" emotionally in very primitive ways with little or no thought involved (e.g., "This guy is crazy," "You S.O.B.," "Boy, I'll get you for this,") and that such over-reactions are not interpretable in attributional terms. Overall, Zillmann's analysis is an elaborate analysis of emotional behavior that promises to be a stimulant for broader and more rigorous work on the role of attribution in the production of emotion. The analysis is, however, so complex that empirical work designed to probe its features may be slow in developing, and thus the analysis may not have the type of immediate impact associated with Schachter and Singer's initial work.

A Brief Comentary on the Significance of these Advances and Extensions

In chapter 3, we will review major critical analyses of attributional concep-tions. But at this point, it is necessary to comment generally and briefly about the advances and extensions that have been reviewed in this chapter.

These statements represent the major theoretical movements in the attribution area after the early foundation work reviewed in chapter 1 (with the exception of Schachter and Singer's work which, as noted above, was not originally con-ceived as an attributional model). They reveal the great breadth and flexibility of attributional analysis applied in varying contexts and to varying types of human action. They reveal in a clear and major way the impact attributional theorizing has had upon social psychology. These advances and extensions were borne out of the early theoretical work, but the advances and extensions, too, have now led to extensive research and writing.

On the other hand, these and other recent advances and extensions have been criticized because they represent too little of an "advance" beyond the early theoretical work. For example, Jones and Kelley (1978) emphasized the fact that numerous attributional theories had emerged but that little theoretical work on basic psychological processes involved in attributions had been done. Essen-tially, they argued there had been too much application of earlier ideas and development of mini-theories for various phenomena and too little work on fun-damental processes (as is found in Jones and Davis, 1965, and Kelley, 1967). A number of other criticisms also have surfaced, particularly regarding this work during the 1970s. Critics have said that basic terms were not agreed upon in the area (e.g., internal-external dichotomy used by many and the endogenous-ex-ogenous dichtomy used by a few—see Shaver, 1979), that the area is a mélange or patchwork of diffuse ideas and strands of work, and that there are several major irresolvable controversies in the area (e.g., over the role egotism plays in attributional activities).

We will not attempt to analyze the merit of these and other criticisms of developments in the attribution area in recent years. As was argued at the beginning of the book, the area is vast in number of ideas, investigators, assumptions about science, beliefs about where work is necessary, and so on. Consensus is not likely to emerge readily among so many workers and so many interested readers. We do think that the basic process problem is now (in the early 1980s) being redressed, and that some of the inconsistencies and controversies have been argued to the point that the strengths and weaknesses of the positions are fairly apparent. Hence, we believe that there will be another season of major advances and extensions in the 1980s. As Kelley (1978) said when asked about the past and future of attribution work: ". . . it wasn't some bright idea that somebody had, that somebody forced on somebody's data or tried to extend by brute force. It came out of a lot of phenomena that social psychologists have looked at and tried to interpret. I just can't imagine that the phenomena that are hooked into that kind of cognition will change or be modified. They'll never go away. We'll always have to have that kind of explanation" (p. 384).

We are not more ingenious in searching out bad motives for good actions when performed by others than for good motives for bad actions when performed by ourselves.

Charles Caleb Colton
Lacon, 1825.

Critical Analyses of Attribution Assumptions

3

This chapter will address recent works that have called into question various assumptions that underlie attribution conceptions. The works that are available are rather limited in scope probably because of the difficulty of assessing the many and diverse strands of attributional theories in any one work. Topics to be discussed include the extent to which people are aware of the factors that influence them in carrying out social behavior, and the extent to which such behavior is scripted and not governed by conscious thought processes and arguments relating to more specific concepts. We should make it clear from the outset that the most imposing analyses to be discussed below apply to theories in cognitive social psychology. As they picture humans to be thoughtful and deliberate, most theories in this general domain would be subject to challenge by the principal analyses to be discussed. However, attributional conceptions and constituent assumptions are at the center of contemporary cognitive social psychology and, hence, represent a major target of these critical analyses.

Central to this chapter is the question of how aware people are of the various and often complex attributions they make about others—especially significant others—in their lives. How aware is Bob that after six weeks of dating Sally he has developed an interpretation of Sally as an arrogant, selfish person who is never likely to be very good for him? Are people sometimes highly deliberate and thoughtful in making these attributions (as, for example, Kelley, 1967, would suggest)? Or are they only somewhat deliberate and *aware* (as Kelley, 1972a, would suggest)? Or are they very much unaware, as some of the theorists to be mentioned in this chapter might suggest? A conclusion that we will nurture in this chapter is that each of these possibilities may be true under certain conditions. The important task is to discover those conditions.

Limitations in Cognitive-Attributional Capabilities

Awareness of Cognitive Processes and Influencing Variables

An analysis about people's cognitive shortcomings was presented by Nisbett and Wilson (1977). These theorists were concerned about how thoughtful people indeed are in making attributions and predictions, forming judgments and so on. In fact, they were quite skeptical about traditional conceptions regarding people's rather ample capabilities. Nisbett and Wilson offered three general arguments that may be paraphrased from their statement (p. 233) as follow:

1. People often cannot report accurately on the effects of particular stimuli on higher-order, inference based responses. Further, they sometimes cannot report on critical stimuli that affect them, their responses to such stimuli, or the processes (such as attribution) intervening between stimuli and responses. Nisbett and Wilson say, "The accuracy of subjective reports is so poor as to suggest that any introspective access that may exist is not sufficient to produce generally correct or reliable reports" (p. 233).
2. When reporting on the effects of stimuli, people may not use a memory of the intervening cognitive processes that were influenced by the stimuli. Rather, they may base their reports on implicit, causal theories about the connection between stimulus and response. These theories are similar to causal schemata in Kelley's (1972a) analysis. For example, "They had that terrible fight because she had had a rough day, and he then came home and pestered her." This attribution corresponds generally to a multiple cause schema people might hold for explaining "terrible fights." According to Nisbett and Wilson, there are various other types of implicit causal theories, and they mostly are ideas we learn to hold through our daily experiences and societal norms.
3. Finally, subjective reports about higher mental processes are sometimes correct, but even the instances of accuracy are not due to introspective awareness. Instead, these correct reports are due to the incidentally correct employment of a priori causal theories such as those mentioned above.

Before discussing Nisbett and Wilson's position further, and criticisms of that position, a number of general comments about the analysis are necessary. First, it is notable that Nisbett and Wilson seem to be adopting an "anti-introspectionist" position (Rich, 1979). Arguments favoring either introspection or anti-introspection positions frequently were presented in the early part of the twentieth century when the science of psychology was being developed. While such arguments have not been so common in recent years, Nisbett and Wilson have helped rekindle interest in the role of introspection in experimental psychology. Not unlike Bem's (1967b, 1972) well-known arguments, Nisbett and Wilson's analysis is a stirring polemical work that involves *a degree* of logical and empirical support and that has received notice throughout the field of psychology.

The general import of Nisbett and Wilson's analysis for attribution conceptions derives from the fact that many of the major conceptions (e.g., Heider,

1958; Jones & Davis, 1965; Kelley, 1967) at least imply awareness, and probably some degree of accuracy, in people's attributional activities in terms of their knowledge of what general factors are affecting them and how they are responding on a behavioral and cognitive level. It is important to note, however, that the major attributional formulations do not imply that there is complete awareness or a high degree of accuracy. Very definitely, Nisbett and Wilson are arguing for a limited attributional capacity on the part of the human organism. Also, they are arguing that what attributional activity does occur is not as thoughtful and extemporaneous as has been suggested in most major theoretical statements.

We would call the reader's attention to qualifiers such as "often," "sometimes," and "may" found in the first but not the latter part of Nisbett and Wilson's general arguments presented above. This tendency to qualify parts of the analysis and not others also is found in the statement as a whole. The reader need be "aware" (ironically so—in light of Nisbett and Wilson's thesis) lest the lack of qualification be taken to mean that Nisbett and Wilson have made a strong case. As we will see below, such a conclusion is not tenable at this time.

An Illustrative Study

Nisbett and Wilson reviewed a number of studies which they claim fail to provide evidence about the people's processing of relevant stimuli or mediational conditions. We will review briefly their argument for one attribution-related study. In a study by Nisbett and Schachter (1966), subjects were requested to take a series of electric shocks of steadily increasing intensity. Before being exposed to the shock, some of the subjects were given a placebo pill which, they were told, would produce various arousal symptoms such as heart palpitations. Nisbett and Schachter expected that when subjects with these instructions were exposed to the shock, they would attribute their arousal symptoms to the pill and thus would tolerate more shock than would subjects who could only attribute these symptoms to the shock. This expectation was strongly borne out in the results. After subjects participated, they were interviewed to see if they could explain their tendencies to take more or lesser degrees of shock. They reported little awareness. This unawareness held even when placebo pill subjects were asked if they thought the pill was causing some effects. Only three out of twelve subjects reported having made the postulated attribution of arousal to the pill, and in general the subjects did not believe they had followed the thought sequence specified by the hypothesis when it was explained to them.

Criticism of Nisbett and Wilson's Position

Nisbett and Wilson used this evidence from Nisbett and Schachter as well as results from other studies to suggest that generally no association has been found between the degree of verbal report change and degree of behavior change in experimental groups. Their argument is intriguing. However, a number of questions about the argument may be raised. For example, the probing of thought (or interviewing) may have been insensitive to the process-related cognitions subjects entertained during the experiment. In the case of Nisbett and Schachter's subjects, they may have thought more about the pill than they admitted, yet were too embarrassed or unsure of their logic to admit their thoughts to the experimenter in the postexperimental debriefing. Furthermore, people's ability to articulate reasoning processes (especially in an interview with a stranger-experimenter) may differ from their actual experience of such reasoning.

Critical commentaries on Nisbett and Wilson's analysis have been provided by Smith and Miller (1978), Rich (1979), Bowers (1979), and White (1980). Smith and Miller suggested that Nisbett and Wilson's position cannot be readily refuted or properly tested. According to Smith and Miller, Nisbett and Wilson appear to regard as illustrative of their position both correct and incorrect accounts by subjects of their reasoning processes. As Smith and Miller noted, the Nisbett-Wilson argument consists in part of a series of studies in which subjects are unable to report the influence of effective stimulus factors. In one of their studies, Nisbett and Wilson had subjects memorize word pairs under the cover of a psychological experiment. Some of the word pairs (e.g., "ocean-moon") were intended to generate associations that would show up in the form of particular responses to a later, ostensibly unrelated task. For instance, subjects exposed to the word pair "ocean-moon" should be more likely than control subjects to name "Tide" when later requested to name a laundry detergent; this effect was expected because people probably have built up a fairly strong association for ocean-moon and tide or an image of the moon over the ocean and tide. These associative effects did in fact appear. However, subjects generally did not report that their responses were influenced by the memorization task. Nisbett and Wilson advanced such evidence as support for their position. But as Smith and Miller contended, "Nisbett and Wilson . . . are implicitly using an impossible criterion for introspective awareness: that subjects be aware of what we systematically and effectively hide from them by our experimental design . . . a between-subjects design like the Tide study makes it impossible for the subject to know what is being experimentally varied and what is being held constant" (p. 256). White (1980) essentially reinforced these methodological criticisms and provided further arguments about the insensitivity of the methods Nisbett and Wilson employed.

Rich's (1979) analysis challenged the explanatory value of Nisbett and Wilson's emphasis upon people's use of implicit causal theories in making inferences. According to Nisbett and Wilson, causal theories are developed from implicit and explicit cultural rules, generalized covariation information, and overlapping connotative networks. If these theories have powerful influences upon individuals, true covariations between causes and effects may go undetected by these individuals, and covariations may be perceived where none are present as a result of incorrect theory applications. But, as Rich suggests, "If several theories could potentially account for the same event, is there any reason why one explanation is superior to others? If theories lead to inappropriate interpretations—failing to detect covariation or perceiving covariation where none is present—how are errors recognized and theories improved or modified? . . . Nisbett and Wilson seem to have portrayed an inflexible stereotypic decision maker" (p. 31).

Bowers' (1979) commentary is perhaps the most potent of these critical analyses of Nisbett and Wilson's position. In addition to touching on points such as those mentioned above, Bowers argues that if the causes of behavior are necessarily and automatically as accessible to people as they in fact are influential in affecting behavior, then there would be no need for psychology. People would, in such a case, know all that there is to know about human behavior; hence, why would we need to investigate human behavior? The answer to this rhetorical but compelling line of reasoning is that people cannot possibly always know the causes of their behavior. They may have an understanding that more or less parallels that of the scientist. But even the scientist's causal understanding is probably incomplete and subject to revision. Thus, in this conception, Nisbett and Wilson's intrigue about people's limitations regarding introspective access to understanding of their behavior is puzzling—how could people not be so limited? Bowers' analysis also leads to a stance that Nisbett and Wilson may have developed some leads about a theory of the unconscious determinants of behavior. Bowers recommends a continuation of that development which will likely involve examination of a question stated early in this discussion, namely: When and why are people highly aware, less aware, or not aware of the influences on their behavior? We certainly would endorse this development in both theoretical and empirical realms, and we view the debate stimulated by Nisbett and Wilson's analysis as having virtually ended, with the general conclusion being that considerable logical, theoretical, and empirical work is necessary before further advances will occur in our understanding of people's awareness of their own mental processes.

The Consensus Controversy

Another debate stimulated by Nisbett and his colleagues concerned the extent to which people's attributions are influenced by consensus information. It will be recalled from Chapter 1 that in Kelley's (1967) ANOVA model, consensus is one of the validating criteria people are assumed to use in making causal judgments. One prediction, for example, that follows from the ANOVA model and that has received empirical support (e.g., Orvis, Cunningham, & Kelley, 1975) is that behavior low in consensus (i.e., few others exhibit the same behavior) produces attribution to the actor. Although previous to the debate there was evidence in the literature that people use consensus information in making causal attributions, Nisbett and his colleagues fostered this debate with a series of studies revealing little evidence to support the consensus prediction. This controversy about consensus occurred prior to Nisbett and Wilson's statement. However, Nisbett et al.'s position on consensus fits well with the work on awareness and in fact constitutes a subclass of the set of effects which these theorists have called into question. In our review, we will selectively discuss the evidence and arguments advanced by Nisbett et al. and some of the vast amount of subsequent work that essentially leads to the conclusion that consensus effects are stronger under some conditions than others.

Early Research by Nisbett and Colleagues

Nisbett, Borgida, Crandall, and Reed (1976) presented evidence which they interpreted to mean that people are relatively insensitive to consensus information in making predictions and attributions but that they often do use small, possibly nonrepresentative cases in their inferences. Nisbett et al. linked their ideas about representativeness to the literature on the psychology of judgment prediction. Presumably, people accord little weight to general population statistics (e.g., about the link between drinking and automobile death); however, they give considerable weight in their judgments to singular but vivid and often personal facts (e.g., the death of a friend who had been drinking in a car wreck).

In one of their studies, Nisbett et al. found that subjects were no more likely to infer that a target member of a population behaved in an extreme way (e.g., gave another person high levels of electric shock) when they knew that extreme behavior was common for the population than when they knew that extreme behavior was atypical. However, subjects were willing to infer that typical behavior for a population was extreme when they were told that a sample of as few as two cases (described in vivid, concrete terms) behaved in an extreme way. Finally, it was found that subjects' judgments about the role of an individual's dispositional qualities in producing his/her extreme behavior were unaffected by knowledge that extreme behavior was typical in the situation. Nisbett and his colleagues suggested that both attributions and predictions may be based upon certain types of logically weak (though very concrete) information and are not sensitive to certain types of logically compelling information.

In another set of studies, Nisbett and Borgida (1975) found no evidence that consensus affects attributions. In one of these studies, they gave subjects a description of a study of helping behavior carried out by Darley and Latané (1968). After receiving the description, subjects were provided with the results of the study (the consensus information). For example, some were told that of fifteen persons witnessing an epileptic seizure six failed to do anything to help; other subjects were not given this information. Then subjects were told that one of the subjects, Greg R. never helped the person suffering the seizure. Subjects were asked to explain Greg R.'s behavior by indicating to what extent the situation or Greg R.'s personality had been the cause of his behavior. The consensus information was effective in the sense that the subjects receiving the information indicated that more participants in the study of helping never helped than did subjects given no information However, consensus had no effect on attribution about Greg R.'s behavior; subjects exhibited no significant differences in attributing Greg R.'s behavior to the situation or his personality. Based on reasoning from Kelley's (1967) analysis, it would have been expected that subjects would attribute Greg R.'s behavior more to the situation in the high consensus (i.e., where six people never helped) condition than in the no consensus information condition. Nisbett and Borgida concluded that ". . . base rate information [such as consensus data] concerning categories in a population is *ignored* in estimating category membership of a sample of the population" (p. 935) [our emphasis].

Qualifying Research

After these early investigations, several studies appeared showing that under certain conditions, consensus effects could be found for both predictions and attributions. In particular, these studies challenged the extreme position that people totally "ignore" base rate or consensus information in making judgments. The resulting dialogue between advocates of the original position that consensus has little or no effect versus advocates of the position that under certain conditions consensus effects are likely to be found is epitomized in articles by Wells and Harvey (1977), Borgida (1978), and Wells and Harvey (1978). Some salient aspects of this work will be reviewed below.

Wells and Harvey (1977) replicated Nisbett and Borgida's (1975) main findings, but also reported relatively strong effects on predictions and attributions for different operationalizations of consensus. The different variations used by Wells and Harvey were designed to indicate that participants in the original studies used by Nisbett and Borgida (e.g., Greg R. in the study of helping) were *representative* of the general population of college students and involved new and more extreme levels of consensus information (e.g., relatively low and high numbers of participants who helped the person having the epileptic seizure). The data showed especially high attribution to the situation the more representative the participants and the higher the level of consensus. Wells and Harvey contended that the representativeness variable reduced the possibility that subjects would have thought the sample to be biased. Also, they suggested that consensus is more potent in its effect at more extreme levels.

The articles by Borgida (1978) and Wells and Harvey (1978), as well as an extensive review of this whole line of work by Kassin (1979), are instructive in revealing what probably are the final conclusions regarding the consensus controversy. Borgida argued that Wells and Harvey's (1977) own data showed prominent underutilization of consensus information in making predictions and attributions. Wells and Harvey admitted as much but noted that an underutilization is not the same as an ignoring of information. Wells and Harvey had built their case on the premise that statistically significant results for the effects of consensus on judgments represented evidence of "use" of consensus information. Borgida (1978), however, explicitly argued that the relatively precise normative model that applies in work on the psychology of prediction should constitute the touchstone for investigators' conclusions about when people utilize consensus or base rate evidence. The normative model is concerned with whether or not people make optimal use of consensus information, as opposed to the statistical model which is concerned with whether or not a significant or non-chance effect was obtained (see Fischhoff, 1976). Clearly, no investigator in this controversy suggested that people exhibit perfect or optimal utilization of information in making judgments. Thus, as of Borgida's (1978) statement, the issue of whether or not people ignore—in a literal sense—consensus information no longer persisted. They do not. They use this information, especially under certain conditions that have been specified in some detail. But they do not use the information precisely—as a computer might—in line with perfect analysis of sample relative to population evidence.

Overall, the consensus controversy has produced an extensive literature revealing conditions when this type of information is used in making attributions, as well as conditions in which it appears to be relatively impotent. Simple conclusions cannot be drawn regarding the impact of consensus relative to the impact of other types of information (consistency, distinctiveness, or whatever). There appear to be situations in which the attributor may utilize one type in deference to others and conditions when combinations of different types of information are differentially utilized (e.g., Hansen & Donoghue, 1977; Orvis, Cunningham, & Kelley, 1975; Ruble & Feldman, 1976).

Script and "Mindlessness" Conceptions

Abelson (1976) and his colleague Langer (1978) have presented provocative accounts of how people may be operating in a highly scripted or even "mindless" way in carrying out certain complex sequences of actions. Of course, this position can be viewed as in opposition to the attributional characterization of the individual as operating often like an intuitive scientist and highly "mindful" in much activity. Abelson and Langer argued that larger units of varied behavior can be chunked together to form fewer coherent cognitive units that are capable of being *overlearned* (e.g., the acts leading to the flushing of a toilet). These units are called *scripts*. To Abelson (1976), a script is "a coherent sequence of events expected by the individual, involving him either as a participant or as an observer" (p. 33); presumably, a script involves a relatively limited amount of cognitive activity. He proposed that there are features abstracted from many single vignettes (e.g., the images of an event that has recently occurred), the basic ingredient of scripts, that help group similar experiences and also help differentiate contrasting ones. With experience on the part of the individual, these features come to be processed instead of the original vignette or vignettes; hence, in this view, "mindlessness" has taken the place of helpful, planful, deliberative inferential activity. Scripts are similar to the a priori causal theories hypothesized by Nisbett and Wilson in that they are assumed to bias individuals to expect certain sequences of events and to promote stereotypic responding on the part of individuals. They also bear some similarity to the concept of causal schemata (Kelley, 1972a). Both scripts and schemata are presumed to be overlearned and to represent processes that occur in a relatively spontaneous way.

Recent work by Langer and her colleagues (Langer, Blank, & Chanowitz, 1978; Langer & Newman, 1979) provides some empirical evidence relevant to the script-mindlessness position. Langer et al. conducted three field experiments to test whether or not behavior often is accomplished without the individual's paying attention to the substantive details of the environment; that is, they were interested in examining the individual's ability to abide by the particulars of a situation without mindful reference to those particulars. In one of these studies, subjects were persons using a copying machine at a large university. When a subject approached the machine, a nearby experimenter asked the subject to allow the experimenter to use the machine first to copy either five or twenty pages. The experimenter's request was made in one of three ways:

1. Request only. "Excuse me, I have 5 (20) pages. May I use the xerox machine?"
2. Placebic information. "Excuse me. I have 5 (20) pages. May I use the xerox machine, because I have to make copies?"
3. Real information. "Excuse me. I have 5 (20) pages. May I use the xerox machine because I'm in a rush?"

The dependent measure was whether or not subjects complied with the experimenter's request. Langer et al. argued that if subjects were processing the information communicated by the experimenter, compliance would be similar for the request only and placebic information groups since the amount of information is the same for these groups; but compliance should be greater for the real information group since this group received additional information. Langer et al. argued, however, that the following prior script would be used by subjects receiving either placebic or real information: "Favor X + Reason Y → Comply. . . ." (p. 637). Even though information given to the placebic information group was redundant, still it was assumed to facilitate scripted action. Such a script was expected to lead to greater compliance for these groups relative to the request only group. In all groups the more effortful (presumably thought-enhancing) request (20 pages) was expected to yield less compliance than the less effortful request (5 pages).

As predicted, Langer et al. found similar and relatively high compliance for the placebic and real information groups, compared to the request only group when the effort required was low. Also, smaller requests resulted in greater compliance than did larger requests. A final finding was that when the request was large, only the real information condition lead to relatively high compliance—presumably because a large request stimulated thought and thus a more legitimate excuse was necessary for the person to allow the experimenter to use the copying machine.

Langer et al. (1978) did not collect data regarding subjects' thoughts at the time of the request. This omission may be unfortunate because it might have shed light on subjects' causal inferences about the requester's behavior. For example, it seems possible that subjects in the placebic information condition interpreted the "I have to. .. ." construction as informative about the requester (e.g., "He is too wrapped up in his affairs to give a better reason"). If such an interpretation occurred, it may have produced a sense of obligation on the part of the subject receiving the placebic information. Langer et al. (1978), however, probably would dispute this possibility. They suggested that attribution investigators have based their ideas too much on the self-reports of over-aroused laboratory subjects whose behavior would likely be scripted and relatively mindless in naturalistic settings.

Concluding Comments

Similar to the analyses of Nisbett and associates, the work of Abelson, Langer, and colleagues raise questions about the inferential processes traditionally assumed by cognitive social psychology. As has been noted already, this challenge is serious for attributional approaches that tacitly or explicitly assume such processes to be occurring. But as we discussed at some length in the section on the Nisbett et al. work, this approach requires much more empirical attention to substantiate arguments about level or type of cognitive processing occurring, and when scripts-mindlessness are operative versus when they are not. It seems obvious that much cognitive-attributional activity can be expected in some situations (e.g., when one is experiencing difficulty in interpersonal relations), and advocates of the approach need to present evidence relevant to these "highly mindful" situations as well as the ones where mindlessness may be evident. Langer (1978) does provide a set of suggestions regarding when people will engage in thought versus when they will not. She included the following among the conditions that may stimulate thought:

1. When people encounter a novel situation for which they have no script.
2. When enacting scripted behavior becomes effortful, i.e., when significantly more of the same kind of scripted behavior is demanded by the situation than was demanded by the original script. This situation may exist when a person performs a monotonous assembly-line task, but then as time goes on, the person has to develop additional scripted (and even more monotonous) routines—possibly leading to a "dawning recognition" that the job is not worth the pay.
3. When enacting scripted behavior is interrupted by external factors that do not allow for its completion.
4. When the situation does not allow for sufficient involvement. For example, a spectator at a dull baseball game on a long summer day may mentally become uninvolved in the game and engrossed in thoughts about personal affairs.

While provocative, these suggestions have not as yet received empirical test.

Causes and Reasons

Similar to the arguments that developed about consensus information, there have been other specific arguments directed at basic attribution assumptions. In one such commentary, Buss (1978) suggested that attribution theorists have not distinguished between causes and reasons. Similar to Kruglanski's (1975) conception of the endogenous-exogenous dichtomy described in Chapter 2, Buss contended that a cause is something which brings about a change, while a reason is something for which a change is brought about (e.g., goals, purposes, etc.).

Buss offered these propositions:

The major cases involving reason explanations of human action include (a) justifying, evaluating, or appraising the action; (b) stating the goal, end, or intention of the action; and (c) stating the means or instrumentality of the goal, end, or intention of the action. All of these reason-type explanations help to make an action intelligible by attaching meaning to the action. . . . By causal explanation one refers to lawfulness and predictability. . . . Causes are necessary when dealing with either (a) unintelligible or irrational intended behavior or (b) unintended behavior (Buss, 1978, p 1314).

Buss also contended that actors and observers differ in the types of explanations they may give for actions and occurrences. He hypothesized that occurrences were explained with causes by both actors and observers; whereas actions were explained solely with reasons by actors, observers could give reason or causal explanations of actions. Buss offered no evidence to support this hypothesis. Further, given the reasoning behind the actor-observer hypothesis described in Chapter 2, it seems questionable to attribute to the observer, who lacks background information about the actor, the ability to make both reason and causal explanations, whereas, actors can provide only reason explanations.

Buss' statement is useful in emphasizing the import of distinguishing cause and reason explanations in attributional analysis. However, as noted by Harvey and Tucker (1979) and Shaver (in press), such an emphasis may be found without too much difficulty in very early attribution works such as those of Heider (1958) and Jones and Davis (1965). For example, Heider wrote, ". . . we shall use the term intention to refer to *what* a person is trying to do, that is the goal or action outcome, and not to *why* he is trying to do it. The latter applies more particularly to the reasons behind the intention" (1958, p. 110, emphasis in original).

The interested reader is referred to a debate on Buss' analysis that is found in Kruglanski (1979), Harvey and Tucker (1979) and Buss (1979). Thus far, no evidence has been presented to resolve this debate.

Ethogenic Perspective

Finally, we should recognize a few of the arguments about attribution theory and research stemming from the so-called ethogenic perspective. This perspective is especially popular in contemporary British and European social psychology. Ethogenics in part refers to a theoretical emphasis upon people's ordinary explanations of behavior in everyday social life. Harré (in press), a leading figure in the ethogenic school, suggested that attribution theorists have made little progress in their experimental-laboratory dominated approach to the study of people's natural explanation tendencies. He argued that they would do well to study forms of folk-attributions. For example, the investigator might focus on the kinds of attributions that are made in a confessional, both by priest to parishoner, and by the parishoner to those whom he feels he has wronged. Harré argued that experiments are of little value in studying people's common explanations. In his suggestion that the investigator must go beyond the experiment, Harré argued, . . ."if we really understand the knowledge, beliefs and skills that are required for the production of a piece of social life, and an ordinary explanation of it, then we ought to be able to use that knowledge to reproduce it" (p. 23).

Harré and other writers from the ethogenic school (e.g., Shotter, in press) have suggested that their perspective provides a much more realistic account of the naive attributor's explanations than do attributional conceptions. Harré (in press) offered this specific charge about what he viewed as the narrow perspective of attribution theorists: "In order to understand how psychologists might set about explaining the actions of their fellow-actors, including, of course, their own attributions about other folk, we must pay attention to the self-presentational dramaturgy of social psychologists. Social psychologists are no more immune to the contagion of the cognitions they study than are microbiologists against their viruses; the latter, of course, take stringent precautions against infection, but I can see no evidence of this amongst attribution theorists" (p. 7).

The arguments made by Harré and his colleagues in the ethogenic school are provocative. They deserve study by American attribution workers, who generally appear to be unaware of the magnitude and popularity of ethogenic work in England and Europe. But arguments driving from ethogenic writing have not gone without challenge (e.g., see Harris & Harvey, in press). In particular, writers in the ethogenic school appear to be proposing an unfair characterization of attribution theorists when they assert that such theorists do not recognize the reflexivity in the attribution process (i.e., that theorists themselves are making attributions in much the same manner that the subjects of their studies make attributions). Indeed, from the outset of work in the field, attribution theorists appear to have been highly cognizant of the parallels between scientific and naive attributional processes.

Conclusion

As we have seen in this chapter, the most potent challenges to basic attribution assumptions have evolved from arguments concerning people's cognitive limitations. These challenges relate to core attribution assumptions about how individuals are deliberative, analytic, and broad in their inferences about people and events. There are the additional notions that whatever individuals' cognitive capabilities, they often lack awareness of their thought processes and react in habitual, stereotypic ways.

In the future, it seems likely that progress in investigating limitations such as those posited by Nisbett, Abelson, Langer, and others, depends upon careful study of differentiating conditions. At the present time, empirical evidence about such conditions is available only in the area of consensus effects. On the other hand, there appears to be little cogency left in the more specific controversies about consensus and causes and reasons. Finally, the arguments being made by the ethogenic school need much more study and appreciation by American attribution investigators.

Applications

Attributional analyses assume that people are motivated to develop organized, meaningful accounts of the numerous events they observe everyday. People are seen as having a need to explain, predict, and try to control their social environments. The attribution of events to invariances and dispositional properties helps to serve this need. This assumption that individuals are motivated to predict and control their environments is central to each of the chapters in this section.

In the first chapter of this section on applications of attributional analyses, Ben Harris asks whether everyone is equally adept at forming attributions that allow for prediction and control of a complex social environment. The preceding discussions of basic attribution formulations and criticisms of these formulations were concerned with causal inference processes of adults. Harris examines evidence relevant to the attributional activity of young children and to the specification of developmental patterns in the process of attributing responsibility and causality.

In almost every major theoretical analysis of attribution processes, the notions of perceived freedom and control have played important roles—they both have implications for the assignment of responsibility for people's behavior and outcomes. In Chapter 5, we review theory and research concerned with determinants of people's inferences about their own and others' freedom and control and the consequences of these inferences.

In Chapter 6, we examine how attributional processes influence individuals' cognitive, behavioral, and emotional reactions to uncontrollable behavioral outcomes. Specifically, we discuss attributional processes as they relate to Seligman's (e.g., Abramson, Seligman, & Teasdale, 1978) learned helplessness model of depression and to Storms and McCaul's (1976) model of the emotional exacerbation of dysfunctional behaviors.

The last chapter of this section is concerned with the role of attributional processes in the treatment of maladaptive behavior patterns. We examine research relevant to two major forms of attributional treatments of various maladaptive behaviors: misattribution and reattribution training therapies. In addition, we present evidence suggesting that individuals are more likely to maintain treatment improvements if they assume responsibility for their behavioral changes.

Developmental Aspects of the Attributional Process

Ben Harris
Vassar College

If attribution theory relates to humans' attempts to understand a complex social environment, certain questions can be posed: Is everyone equally adept at this task? Do we all adopt a similar style of seeking and interpreting attributional information?

One way of approaching such questions is to note that in most of the preceding discussion, the emphasis has been on the attributions of adults or cognitively mature individuals. Although such emphasis is natural, given the subject populations traditionally studied, it must not blind us to the possibility that adult attributional styles are part of a developmental progression. In other words, we must entertain the question of whether adult patterns of attribution (e.g., the discounting effect) may not be different from the attributional activity of young children. This chapter explores various attempts to answer that question, and to specify developmental patterns in the process of attributing responsibility and causality. In doing so, it focuses on developmental aspects of Heider's (1958) theory, attributionally relevant aspects of Piaget's moral development theory, and the research that both these theoretical statements have helped generate. This account ends by reviewing recent, development studies of Kelley's (1972) discounting principle, and of the related, overjustification effect (Lepper, Greene, & Nisbett, 1973).

The Attribution of Causality and Responsibility

As the reader knows from earlier chapters, attributions of responsibility and causality are only two of many types of attributional activity studied by psychologists. However, this chapter chiefly focuses on causal and responsibility-related attributions, because of their central role in statements of attribution theory (e.g., Heider, 1958; Kelley, 1967) and in subsequent research. With this in mind, it should be acknowledged that there are developmental aspects of other attributional processes not primarily related to social and physical causality or to responsibility. For example, the literature on achievement-related attributions contains studies comparing adults' and children's attributional differences when responding to task-related success and failure (see Guttentag & Longfellow, 1978, for a review). Also, noteworthy research has been done on the development of trait attributions, most often using content analysis of children's descriptions of themselves and of others (see Bromley, 1978; Guttentag & Longfellow, 1978; Livesley & Bromley, 1974; Secord & Peevers, 1974; Calveric, 1979).

The Attribution of Responsibility

In both social and developmental psychology, attributing responsibility for events is a familiar experimental task. Following Walster's influential study of the "assignment of responsibility for an accident," much research by social psychologists was devoted to the cataloguing of situational and subject-related effects on this process (see Shaver, 1970, pp. 106-111). Similarly, developmental psychologists in recent years have shown an increasing interest in the related process of moral judgment, following Piaget's early study of children's perception of the naughtiness of a child involved in a damage-causing accident.

The similarity between what developmentalists call moral judgment and what social psychologists call responsibility attribution makes this an interesting research area. At the same time, it is on an area beset by conceptual difficulties and confusion.

Varieties of Responsibility

A major source of confusion in psychological research on responsibility is the variety of meanings that can be attached to the term "responsibility." In the literature of social psychology, for example, one can find different researchers using the term "attribution of responsibility" to refer to quite different psychological processes. In one experiment this term may refer to causal judgments of the *correspondence* between a person's written essay and his or her attitude on an issue (e.g., see Kruglanski & Cohen, 1973); in another study, attributed responsibility may refer to the judgments of *guilt* made by subjects in simulated judicial decisions (e.g., see Phares & Wilson, 1973).

In order to make sense out of such different uses of the term responsibility, it is important to note that patterns of common language and legal usage for the term responsibility are as complex as the patterns found in psychological use. In all these areas, "responsibility" can refer to attributing simple causality on the one hand, to deciding moral blame or culpability on the other.

In criminal law, one finds that there are two basic types of responsibility which can be assigned for criminal actions, corresponding to two different functions of the legal process. The older, simpler view of responsibility is that the structure of society is codified in laws, which in turn serve as rules for human behavior. If these laws are broken, the social order must be corrected for the good of society; thus, assigning responsibility serves to identify the causal agent for a rupture of the social order (without necessarily any concern for extenuating circumstances). Viewed in this manner, one's "responsibility" for an action is *not* affected by factors such as seriousness of outcome (as in larceny vs. grand larceny), or from motivational differences in an event's execution (as in intentional vs. unintentional acts). Rather, public order must be restored by simply finding the proper causal agent.

In contrast to this view of responsibility as an absolute (mostly causal) characteristic, there is the more modern and utilitarian concept of responsibility as a conditional attribute. Based on the idea that society is best served by increasing individual social productivity, this orientation would have the law not just punishing but also helping each person toward his order most useful social behaviors. In application, this means that assigning responsibility, e.g., to someone named Ralph for a criminal event, would not just be done to restore the social order, but to deter or reform Ralph so that he would not repeat the same action. To this end, the assessment of Ralph's responsibility must be based on an appraisal of his intention, since intention differentiates reformable from non-reformable actions. Thus, the attribution of responsibility for utilitarian ends must include, as a component, the attribution of intent.

This differentiation of types of judicial responsibility could be repeated for other fields, most notably in the area of traditional English usage.[1] However, the above examples sufficiently illustrate two points about the general concept of responsibility. First, there seems to be the potential for much confusion in any setting if one attempts to discuss judgments (or attributions) of responsibility with no specification of context or of special meaning. Second, it seems as if most definitions of responsibility are based on a central core of causality with various degrees of culpability attached; the more that culpability is in question, the more that details of the causal agent (e.g., his or her intention) become salient.

In the review of the literature on responsibility that follows, studies are included if they: (1) use developmental populations, and (2) ask for judgments of blame, naughtiness, culpability, or responsibility for social events. While studies may vary in degree to which they try to examine moral vs. causal judgments, an examination of the experimenter's actual instruction to subjects usually clarifies the concepts being studied.

The Moral Judgment Paradigm of Jean Piaget

To those interested in the development of the attribution of responsibility, Piaget's work *The Moral Judgement of the Child* (1932) has had a singular influence. On the level of methodology, Piaget's technique of eliciting children's attributions to story characters continues to be a feature of recent moral judgment studies, although in modified form. On a theoretical level, Piaget's writing on moral development is equally influential. In it, he describes children's progression from a stage of generally *egocentric morality* to the more relative *morality of reciprocity* (Hoffman, 1970). According to Piaget, the moral judgments of children in these two stages differ in many ways, such as in their evaluation of lying, of the validity of group punishment for individual misconduct, and of the value of cooperation. Of most relevance for attribution theory, however, is a single aspect of Piaget's theory of moral development: children's transition from objective (absolute) to subjective (intention-based) evaluations of social behavior.

According to Piaget, a young child's judgment of the correctness or incorrectness of an act is based on the external, or *objective* characteristics of the actor's behavior. Thus "the child will at first evaluate acts not in accordance with the motive that has prompted them but in terms of their exact conformity with established rules" (Piaget, 1932, p. 107). Contrasted with this objectivist method of moral judgment is the more mature stage of subjective responsibility; in it, children's judgments are based on internal attributes such as intentionality.

To test children's use of objective versus subjective attributes in their moral judgments, Piaget designed a number of pairs of stories, with each pair containing (a) an act based on good intent that caused significant damage, and (b) an act based on malintent (disobedience) that caused a small amount of damage. To illustrate, two of Piaget's story pairs (1932, p. 86) were:

(Good intent, high damage)   vs.   *(Bad intent, low damage)*

Story #1

A. A little boy who is called John is in his room. He is called to dinner. He goes into the dining room. But behind the door there was a chair, and on the chair there was a tray with fifteen cups on it. John couldn't have known that there was all this behind the door. He goes in, the door knocks against the tray, bang go the fifteen cups and they all get broken.

B. Once there was a little boy whose name was Henry. One day when his mother was out he tried to get some jam out of the cupboard. He climbed up on to a chair and stretched out his arm. But the jam was too high up and he couldn't reach it and have any. But while he was trying to get it he knocked over a cup. The cup fell down and broke.

Story #2

A. There was once a little girl who was called Marie. She wanted to give her mother a nice surprise, and cut out a piece of sewing for her. But she didn't know how to use the scissors properly and cut a big hole in her dress.

B. A little girl called Margaret went and took her mother's scissors one day that her mother was out. She played with them for a bit. Then as she didn't know how to use them properly, she made a little hole in her dress.

After hearing each pair of stories, children were asked (in part) to state which child was the naughtier of the two.

Piaget's goal in this was "to find out whether the child pays more attention to motive or a material results." His reasoning was that if responsibility were judged by objective criteria (indicating a less mature stage), the child in the high-damage story would be judged naughtier. What Piaget found was a gradual shift to subjective responsibility as the age of the respondent increased (the children tested ranged from 6 to 10); age 10 seemed to be the upper limit for objective responsibility.

Evaluation of Piaget's Paradigm

From an attributional viewpoint, this work by Piaget is both provocative and frustratingly incomplete. It is provocative in its suggestion that *adults' interest in dispositional attributes* (Heider, 1944; Ross, 1977) *may not be shared by attributors of all ages.* More specifically, Piaget's work suggests that as observers of others' acts, young children ignore the other's intention when determining his or her naughtiness. The frustration that Piaget's work evokes from some modern attribution theorists is due to its failure to specify the mechanism(s) responsible for this effect. This stems mostly from Piaget's lack of interest in clearly manipulating the attribute of intentionality.

In Piaget's paradigm, the question is being asked of the relative importance of intentionality versus outcome of an act. Suited to this question is a confounding of outcome and intention in the stimulus materials to which the children react. In these stimulus stories, low damage is always associated with malintent and high damage with good intent. Thus, if a child judges John to be naughtier than Henry (Story IA versus IB above), it is impossible to say whether this is due to John's (good) intention being ignored or to the powerful influence of the (damage causing) outcome of his door opening. In other words, from Piaget's (1932) study of moral judgments, there are at least four different interpretations of why young children do not use the attribute of intentionality in naughtiness: either (a) they can not differentiate it from unintentionality, (b) they can differentiate it but do not use it to judge naughtiness, (c) they differentiate it and use it, and weigh it more than outcome, but it is not clearly contained in Piaget's stories (e.g., reaching for jam is not a clearly malintentioned act).

Recent Studies of Children's Use of Intentionality in Attributing Responsibility

Fortunately, the methodological problems with Piaget's early work have been widely acknowledged (see Imamoglu, 1976; Karniol, 1978; Keasey, 1978), and there have been many recent attempts to modify the basic Piagetian paradigm (see Keasey, 1978, for a review of studies within this paradigm). The basic goal of these modifications has been to more directly assess children's attention to intentionality in social events, using a variety of populations, stimulus measures, and dependent measures.

The basic plan of recent studies of children's attributions of intention is seen in Armsby's "reexamination of the developments of moral judgments in children" (1971). The most important feature of this study was the author's independent manipulation of intention and outcome in the stories to which experimental subjects reacted. This was accomplished by constructing separate stories containing either unintentional or intentional acts, with each act paired with one of four different amounts of damage (e.g., breaking one cup, 15 cups, all the plates in a house, or a television). A second noteworthy feature of Armsby's method was his care in making the damage-causing act itself the locus of the actor's intentionality or unintentionality—something not done by Piaget or by many contemporary researchers (see Karniol, 1978, on this point).

Using these simple modifications of Piaget's paradigm, Armsby found the same developmental trend as Piaget (increasing use of intention) but at a much earlier age: a full 75% of the sample of 6 year olds based their attribution of naughtiness on the subjective attribute of intentionality. Subsequent research on the attribution of intention has generally supported Armsby's findings, while also exploring the effects of certain stimulus variables and methodological refinements. One such variable is the mode by which stimulus events are presented to experimental subjects. In most of the literature, experimenters present stories orally or in written format (e.g., Armsby, 1971); however, stimulus events have also been acted out and presented on either film (King, 1971), or on videotape (e.g., Farnill, 1974). Although Chandler, Greenspan, and Barenboim (1973) found evidence that videotaped stories produced more intention-based attributions than stories which were read to subjects, Brendt and Brendt (1975) failed to replicate this finding.

A second variation in the methodology used in some experiments concerns the way in which subjects' attributions are elicited. Although many experiments follow the Piagetian tradition of forced-choice selection from multiple pairs of stimulus stories, some ask subjects to rate the goodness or badness of actors in individual stories (e.g., on a five point scale—Costanzo, Coie, Grumet & Farnill, 1973). While there is reason to believe that such a procedure might change subject's patterns of attribution, the evidence on this point is ambiguous (Berg-Cross, 1975; see Keasey, 1978 for a discussion).

A third methodological issue in this literature involves the salience of intention information compared to information about outcome. If youngest children have the most trouble coding story events (Copple & Coon, 1977), it is reasonable to think that their memory might show a recency effect and thus they might selectively remember more outcome-relevant information (since it is usually presented last—see Piaget's stories above). Evidence supporting this idea has been found by Nummedal and Bass (1976), and many experimenters attempt to minimize such memory-based artifacts by giving children pictorial or written summaries of stimulus events (e.g., Armsby, 1971).

Effects of Outcome on the Attribution of Responsibility

Taking advantage of the many methodological refinements discussed above, investigators have made it possible to validate and independently test for the effects of intention and outcome on children's attribution of responsibility. As already noted, the use of information about others' intentions can be found in children as young as six years old (given the right conditions), and seems to increase slightly with age—both when assessed by responsibility attribution (Armsby, 1971) or more directly (King, 1971). In a complementary fashion, the effect of outcome severity (e.g., the amount of damage caused by an act) on children's moral judgments decreases with age (Armsby, 1971). In combination, these factors of intention and outcome interact to produce the pattern of results that Piaget first described: when evaluated by 5–10 year olds, an event's outcome (e.g., the amount of damage) can mask the effects of its perpetrator's intention.

Although the reason for this finding is unclear (see Karniol, 1978), its reliability is well established. As analyzed by Keasey (1978), there is a developmental trend in the ability of outcome information to mask children's use of intentionality information. For youngest children, the use of intentionality is inhibited by the presence of any information about events' consequences (whether good, bad, or neutral). Later, children's use of intentionality cues is masked by outcome information that varies across events, although not by consistent consequences. Finally, the oldest children can make intention-based attributions independently of any outcome of the events being judged.

Heider's Concept of Attributed Responsibility

To social psychologists, most developmental research on moral judgment is marked by a relatively narrow view of the attributes contained in a social event. Research on Piaget's subjective/objective realism distinction, for example, selects the intentionality of an event as its most developmentally significant attribute. Although intentionality is an important cue for making social attributions (e.g., attributions of responsibility), there is no reason to assume that other characteristics of an event are not equally important.

For those interested in developmental variations of a variety of social attributes, Heider's (1958) theory of interpersonal attribution has provoked much interest. As noted in Chapter 1, Heider's theory involves a cataloguing of the personal and environmental attributes (e.g., task difficulty, carelessness) that affect naive observers' judgment of causality and responsibility. Of most relevance to developmentalists, Heider also speculated briefly on possible developmental trends in the utilization of the attributes which he has described.

The developmental aspect of Heider's theory consists of two basic ideas. First is the hypothesis that one can arrange all social attributes along a dimension of personal/environmental responsibility, with responsibility judged by highly internal attributes (e.g., stable personality characteristics) at one end, and highly external attributes (e.g., environmental coercion) at the other. Heider's second basic idea is that, given an actor in a social environment, observers' judgments of the actor's responsibility for the event may show an age-related developmental progression. This progression is hypothesized to begin with the use of external (environmental) criteria in attributions of responsibility and end with the use of internal, personal attributes for such attributions.

In outlining these ideas, Heider specified five steps or *levels* of responsibility attribution along the personal/environmental dimension already mentioned. At the lowest of these levels, one attributes responsibility for an event to a person based on external, or "local," criteria such as the superficial association between the person and the event. At intermediate levels of attribution of responsibility, one attributes responsibility based on less immediate criteria such as the physical ability of the stimulus person and the estimated difficulty of the stimulus event. Finally, at the level of highest sophistication one's attribution of responsibility responds mainly to the "remote" relevance of the event, based on attributes such as the stimulus person's dispositional character.

Heider (1958) described five specific levels of responsibility ordered in this manner:

I. The first level is that of *association,* marked by the attribution of responsibility to a person "P" for any event that he is in any way associated with. For example, a person named Fred could be held responsible for an event caused in his presence or for an act unknown to him caused by a relative of his. At this level the question "who is responsible for event x?" could be rephrased as "whose existence is in any way connected with the cause of x?"

II. The next level is one of *commission,* or simple causality. At this level, a person must be a necessary cause of an event to elicit an observer's attribution of responsibility for the event's outcome. At this level, for example, Fred would be held responsible for the collapse of a chair that he sat on, even if he could not have foreseen and did not intend the collapse. At this level the question "who is responsible for event x?" could be rephrased by "who was an instrumental cause of event x?"

III. The third level is one of *foreseeability,* characterized by the attribution of responsibility to a person for acts that he caused and could have foreseen, however unintentional the outcome. At this level, for example, Fred would be held responsible for a fire caused by his smoking in bed, because the outcome of Fred's smoking is considered foreseeable by the average person. At this level, the question "who is responsible for event x?" could be translated by "who was a cause of the foreseeable event x?"

IV. The fourth level is that of *intention,* or personal causality, at which point an individual is held responsible only for all intentional acts that he performs. For example, Fred would be held responsible for shooting his hunting partner if and only if he actually intended to injure that person when he pulled the trigger. Thus, the question "who is responsible for event x?" is equivalent at this level to the question "who intentionally caused event x?"

V. The final level is that of justification, or *free commission,* based on the criterion of non-coercive environment. For example, Fred is held responsible at this level for writing a ransom note only if he is not forced into it by a kidnapper (e.g., having a gun pointed at his head while he is writing a ransom note). Similarly, if Fred is starving he is *not* held responsible for attacking someone carrying some food home from the market. At this level the question "who is responsible for event x?" means "who has caused event x in correspondence with his actual dispositions?"

In looking at these levels of increasingly sophisticated responsibility, it should be noted that Piaget's distinction between objective and subjective judgments is similar to the distinction between attributed responsibility at level II or III and level IV. Thus, one can see Heider and Piaget roughly agreeing on the direction followed by moral development, with Heider taking a broader view of the possible stages involved.

Testing Heider's Theory of Attributional Development

There have been three major attempts to test Heider's (1958) developmental theory. The first consisted of related studies by M. Shaw and colleagues, the most noteworthy experiment being conducted by Shaw and Sulzer (1964). Since Shaw's general method of operationalizing and testing Heider's levels has been the basis for all subsequent research in this area, it deserves examination at some length.

Shaw and Sulzer (1964) attempted to test developmental aspects of Heider's theory of levels of attributed responsibility and also to test how an adult population responds to situations with different causal attributes (e.g., intentionality, foreseeability, commission). Their method was to present verbally to two groups of subjects (second graders aged 6–9 years and college students aged 19–38 years), stories of interpersonal events involving a person named Perry. Each story described an event containing the minimum attributes necessary for determining responsibility at one of the five levels described above. For instance, a level II story involved an unforeseeable accident by Perry, while a level III story involved a foreseeable accident, and the corresponding level IV story involved a similar but intentional (non-accidental) act by Perry. Each subject heard two stories appropriate to each level, and for each story subjects were asked to rate Perry's degree of responsibility for the event's outcome.

In employing this methodology, Shaw and Sulzer's assumption was that a particular subject would attribute the most responsibility to Perry in the stories the characteristics of which were appropriate for the subject's level of attributional sophistication. For instance, if college students' attributions were based mostly on intentionality (level IV), they would be expected to attribute the greatest amount of responsibility to Perry in level IV and V stories, since these stories would best establish the criterion of intentional behavior. Similarly, second graders (accepting Piaget's assumption that they attribute at level II) would attribute responsiblity more or less equally in stories at all levels since these stories would all satisfy the level II criterion of simple causality. Consistent with this reasoning, Shaw and Sulzer (1964) found suggestive evidence for the proposition that there are developmental levels of responsibility attribution, although not necessarily in the form suggested by Heider's levels (1958) or by the authors. They found that for subjects' attributions, there was a significant interaction between the effects of subject population (second graders versus college students) and level of stimulus theory. Unfortunately, Shaw and Sulzer failed to report comparisons of subjects' attributions to specific stimulus levels; thus there was no evidence of specific patterns of developmental effects.

In addition to not evaluating the specifics of Heider's hypothesis, Shaw and Sulzer's selection of subject groups and preparation of stimulus stories seem to have resulted in a seriously confounded design. In the case of forming subject groups, the large difference in age between the two groups of subjects necessitates a demonstration that the stimulus stories were equally comprehended by both groups. Without this demonstration the possibility exists that the "children" understood all the stories equally poorly, while the "adults" were familiar enough with the vocabulary and instructions to distinguish one story from another. According to this possibility, the interaction between the stimulus levels and population found by Shaw and Sulzer could be the simple result of the "children" attributing relatively low amounts of responsibility in a constant manner independent of the stimuli and the "adults" attributing responsibility in accordance with the stimulus demands. With five levels of stimulus stories and two levels of the populations available, this might produce data similar to those found by the authors.

Shaw and his associates (Shaw & Iwawaki, 1972; Shaw & Schneider, 1969; Shaw, Bristoe & Garcia-Esteve, 1968) have subsequently performed a number of studies using subjects grouped by age, and stimulus stories similar to those of Shaw and Sulzer (1964). Although these studies all produced significant interaction effects of subjects' age and the stimulus stories, there were again no specific comparisons reported by the authors between the attributional patterns of one age group versus another. In addition, the stimulus material used by Shaw and his associates in all of these studies may not have clearly reflected Heider's five levels of responsibility. For instance, the theoretical difference between a level III and a level IV story is the *intentionality* of the target person's behavior. Although the level III and level IV stories in Shaw's AR questionnaire do differ in intentionality, they also differ in other respects. One of Shaw's level III stories is:

Perry was taking his little sister to school. She started to step into a busy street but Perry wanted to look in a store window, so he pulled her back. This kept his sister from being hit by a speeding car.

and the equivalent level IV story is:

Perry was fishing when he saw a boy drowning in the river. Perry could not swim, but he fought his way out to the boy and pulled him out.

Not only do these stories differ in the intentionality of Perry's action, but also in his effort and ability—the level IV action is one in which Perry's extremely high effort compensates for his lack of a relevant ability, while the level III action involved low effort and adequate ability. Because of the confounding of intention with effort and ability, any developmental differences in subjects' responses to these stories could not be interpreted as necessarily reflecting the differences in perceiving intentionality that were suggested by Heider (1958). Thus, although the design used by Shaw and his associates may be adequate for testing some of Heider's (1958) idea, there has been a failure to operationalize the relevant variables and perform the statistical tests necessary to investigate developmental differences in the attribution of responsibility.

The second major test of Heider's developmental theory of responsibility attribution was Harris' (1977) attempt to improve on Shaw's stimulus stories and on their method of presentation. This was done by using five videotaped stimulus events that were carefully designed to embody Heider's levels of responsibility. The events all involved the breaking of a chair that was associated with a young girl named Nancy. In the five events, the chair was broken: (I) by someone besides Nancy, (II) by Nancy accidentally, (III) by Nancy-involving a noticeably fragile chair, (IV) by Nancy intentionally, and (V) by Nancy at her mother's request. As in Shaw and Sulzer's study (1964), Harris' subjects were asked to rate Nancy's naughtiness after being exposed to the stimulus events. A unique feature of Harris' study was the use of an exclusively between-subjects design; each subject only saw and rated one stimulus event.

Using groups of subjects from school grades 1, 3, 6, 8, and college, Harris found a pattern of attributions that strongly supported Heider's developmental hypothesis. As Harris had predicted and as Shaw and Sulzer had also found, there was an interaction between the effects of attributor's age and the Heiderian level of the stimulus story (Harris, 1977). Of more importance were the specific comparisons within age groups. As predicted, the groups of more mature attributors showed increased attributions to Nancy as her behavior became more internally caused. By contrast, the groups of less mature attributors showed relatively high, undifferentiated attributions to all stimulus events. In other words, the youngest of Harris' subjects seemed to use more unsophisticated, external criteria when judging another child's responsibility (naughtiness) for an event with a negative outcome.

In a third test of the same hypothesis, Fincham and Jaspars (1979) found similar results. Using children from grades 2, 4, 6 and 8; and with six different types of stimulus stories, childrens' attributions of responsibility ("blame") showed an interaction effect for the variables of subject's age and the level of stimulus story. In general, this took the form of younger children only differentiating one or two of Heider's levels, whereas the attributions of the oldest children were significantly different in response to four of the five levels of the stimulus story.

Compared to Piaget's moral development theory, Heider's work has not generated a great deal of research; it is possible that experimenters have been reluctant to invest the large amount of effort necessary to test a number of different age groups on each of Heider's five levels of responsibility. The studies that have been done, however, are encouraging in their support of Heider's basic view of development; a progression of increasingly sophisticated attributional styles. The next step in this research, it seems, will be to explore in more detail the empirical and conceptual differences between individual pairs of Heider's stages. Such an exploration is necessary to further clarify the mechanism underlying the developmental differences found using a Heiderian paradigm.

The Attribution of Causality

In the studies reviewed so far, children's attributions of responsibility have been the exclusive focus. More specifically, it has been children's assignment of blame that has most often been assessed. Within the broad definition of responsibility proposed above, this is a limited topic for investigation. Within attribution theory as a whole, it is an even narrower focus, since attribution theorists talk most about determining (or "attributing") the causal (rather than moral) properties of events. Of course, attributing blame for an event presupposes some attempt at attribution of causality. However, the dynamics and controlling circumstances of the latter process may be masked by more blame-relevant factors (e.g., outcome—see Keasey, 1978) or by a general moralistic perceptual set (e.g., "situation matching"—see Jones & Thibaut, 1958). Given such variables that influence moral judgments, it is very difficult to tell whether a particular child's failure to utilize a certain social attribute (e.g., forseeability) is due to a failure to perceive it or to a judgmental schema that does not involve its use.

For those interested in the limits of children's ability to use social attributes, the study of causal attribution in a social context provides a more purely cognitive task and one that is less influenced by socialization effects. In general, the development of causal attribution has been studied in two ways. First, it has been related to Heider's levels hypothesis, the major tests of which were described above (Fincham & Jaspars, 1979; Harris, 1977). Second, there has been work on developmental aspects of Kelley's (1972) attribution theory. Specifically, there have been tests of how children develop an understanding of multiple sufficient causes in attributions about others' behavior and about their own.

As described above, Shaw and Sulzer's test of Heider's levels theory exclusively elicited subjects' attribution of responsibility, and did so in a context that may have promoted moral judgments. With this difficulty in mind, both Harris (1977), and Fincham and Jaspars (1979) elicited attributions of causality as well as attributions of responsibility (see above). This was done by eliciting children's *causal* attributions in concert with the assessment of naughtiness. Each child was asked to rate on a scale of increasing causality "How much was [name of actor] the reason for/cause of the [outcome of the event in question]?"

As was expected, assessing children's causal attribution produced a pattern of results generally similar to that elicited by the authors' responsibility measure, but different in certain aspects. In both studies the variables of age and story level interacted to affect perceived causality; however, after stimulus level I there were fewer age-related differences for the measure of causality than for the measure of naughtiness. In the case of Harris' study, this seemed to be due to most subjects' causal criteria being fairly well satisfied when the actor became a necessary cause (levels II–V); by contrast, subjects' criteria for attribution of naughtiness seem to vary much more with age. A roughly similar pattern of results was found by Fincham and Jaspars, with most age groups showing more agreement on causal attributions than on attributions of responsibility.

The results of this comparison of simple causality and moral responsibility suggests that the latter is a more complex concept, such that multiple criteria affect its attribution. Of most relevance to this chapter, these attributional criteria are complex enough to show developmental differences in their utilization, either because this utilization requires mature cognitive processes, or because socialization gradually changes children's rules for the evaluation of (already perceived) attributional cues. Of course, this distinction between causality and responsibility may in reality be more significant than the two studies cited here indicate, since it is very difficult to elicit from young children a measure of "how much is (s)he the cause of that event?" Not only is this a complex concept, but it is difficult to separate from the more familiar concept of naughtiness.

The Development of Attributional Discounting

At its most basic, attribution theory involves the study of how individuals perceive the causes of a particular social event. One of the most valuable concepts in theories of causal attribution has been what Kelley (1972b) terms "the discounting principle." This is the tendency for individuals who are faced with single social events to discount a specific cause when the individual perceives other possible, and equally sufficient causes for the event (see discussion in Chapter 1). In this research, an event, such as person expressing an opinion, is usually described in the context of a strong external cause, such as a bribe. To the extent that this external cause is present, the impact of a possible internal cause (e.g., a stable, personal belief) is found to be *discounted* by the event's observer. As analyzed by Kelley, this effect is a common form of adult causal attribution occurring when an observer is unable, over time, to determine the co-variance of an event and an external cause (see Jones, Davis, & Gergen, 1961). As a frequent process involved in causal attribution, discounting is appropriate for developmental study; unlike most Piagetian tasks previously discussed, it does not involve moral judgments, exclusively negative outcomes, or other potentially confounding factors.

The essential features of developmental studies of the discounting principle can be seen in portions of Baldwin & Baldwin's (1970) experiment on children's judgments of kindness. As part of this study, pairs of illustrated stories were constructed and presented to children ranging from kindergarten to college-age. Of the stories, one pair contrasted adult-requested with spontaneous gift-giving (a child gives his baby brother a toy), whereas another contrasted the spontaneous lending of a toy wagon with lending that followed a brother's promise of a contingent reward. After exposure to these stories, Balwin and Baldwin's subjects selected the òne story from each pair whose actor seemed more kind; subjects' reasons for their selections were then elicited and analyzed. As measured by both the forced-choice question ("which boy is more kind?") and by analysis of subjects' verbal explanation, there were significant differences between kindergarten, second, and fourth grade groups' use of discounting. In general, discounting increased from kindergarten to college age, with a majority of children not discounting internal causes until approximately the fourth grade.

Since Kelley's explicit identification of the discounting principle (Kelley, 1972b), developmental and social psychologists have begun to directly study differences in discounting between groups of children and adults. To assess possible differences in discounting between children in kindergarten, grade 4, and grade 8, Shultz, Butkowsky, Pearce, and Shanfield (1975) developed stories that included an action and either an external or internal cause; subjects were asked to estimate whether a second cause was probably invoved in the already described event. For example, subjects might be given an action such as "Today Johnny is afraid of a dog," and also be given the (internal) cause "Johnny is usually afraid of dogs"; the subjects' task would be to estimate whether another (e.g., external) cause "The dog is very large" is likely to be present in the event. Assessed in this manner, fourth and eighth graders showed significant discounting of both internal and external secondary causes; by contrast, the judgments of kindergarten children about a possible secondary cause were unaffected by the prior establishment of a primary cause.[2] It is noteworthy that although this assessment of discounting by Shultz et al. was methodologically quite different than that of Baldwin and Baldwin, the two studies found discounting to become the preferred attributional style on roughly similar ages.

In another study of discounting, Smith (1975) had children listen to story pairs constructed somewhat differently than those of Baldwin and Baldwin (1970). One of each pair of stories described a child spontaneously selecting one toy to play with, whereas the complementary story described the same behavior following a reward, order, or obligation to play with the toy in question. Using a variety of measurement techniques, Smith assessed children's judgments of the actor's attitude toward the toy with which they played. Consistent with other researchers, Smith found the attributions of fourth graders and college students to show consistent discounting (attributing more toy-liking to the first child), whereas kindergarten children showed essentially none, and second graders showed inconsistent use of this principle.

Although these results are similar to those of experiments already discussed, Smith's methodology does not rule out alternative explanations to an attributional one. As pointed out by Karniol and Ross (1976), presenting story pairs that differ chiefly by the presence or absence of an additional, external cause may elicit effects based on young children's poor memory. Take for example, kindergarten children not differentiating a child's spontaneous play from the child's play following the promise of a reward. In Smith's (1975) experiment, this may have been due to the young subjects' forgetting about the promised reward, rather than because they lacked the ability to use that information to discount a possible internal motive.

To rule out such a memory-based explanation of the developmental of discounting, Karniol and Ross (1976) employed both memory aids and checks of subjects' understanding of each stimulus story. When these procedures were coupled with stories of sanctioned and unsanctioned toy play (similar to Smith's), an interesting result was found. Not only did kindergarten subjects *not* discount internal causes in the presence of external sanctions, but they consistently saw *external causes as indicative of more internal causality!* In other words, when kindergarten children were told about Johnny's sponaneously selecting toy X to play with, and about Gerald's playing with toy X after it was selected for him by his mother, the kindergarten children chose Gerald as the one who "really wanted to play with toy X." Termed the "additive principle" by Karniol and Ross (1976), this effect appears to be replaced by discounting as the child matures (see also Cohen, Gelfand & Hartmann, 1979).

As described by Karniol, the additive principle has two significant implications concerning children's cognitions. It implies, first, that children as young as six do not lack an attributional schema—it may just be one that seems backward to adults. Second, very young children's failure to discount may not be necessarily due to a cognitive inability to decenter (e.g., to pay attention to more than one cause), since the additive principle requires some of this cognitive skill. Rather, Karniol suggests that developmental differences in discounting may be due to different interpretations of adult motives in sanctioning certain play activities. In support of this idea, Karniol and Ross (1979) have recently found evidence that older children often perceive that adult behavior can be a manipulative response to a child's action; that a parent's choice of a toy implies his or her child's rejection of the same toy. If so, then older children's discounting may be based on their attribution of manipulative intent to adults, following these children's belief that parents mostly reward children for doing things that they nomally wouldn't do.

Developing Causal Attribution to Self: The Overjustification Effect

The final attributional phenomenon examined for developmental trends is the overjustification effect. Stated simply, this is an application of Kelley's discounting principle to one's self. If, for example, one engages in two equally pleasant leisure activities such as checkers and dominoes, and one receives an external reward for playing dominoes but not for playing checkers, the overjustification effect would predict an eventual reduction in the one's perceived liking of dominoes compared with checkers. In attributional terms, one's explanation of the event "playing with dominoes" begins to discount "liking dominoes" as a cause.

Studies of the overjustification effect have found consistent behavioral evidence for its operation with children as young as kindergarten-age; such children may show reduced play with a previously interesting toy after they are rewarded for playing with it (Greene & Lepper, 1974; Lepper, Greene & Nisbett, 1973; Ross, 1975; Smith, Gelfand, Hartmann & Partlow, 1979). Although this is not an unexpected phenomenon, it does raise the question of why kindergarten-age children show overjustification in their self-attributions but not discounting in their attributions to others.

Recently, Guttentag and Longfellow (1978) have attempted to explain why children's *self* perceptions show the overjustification effect before discounting is seen in their perception to *others*. These authors first assert that overjustification depends on an over-attention to environmental causes at the expense of internal ones; for example, overattention to one's being rewarded to play with toy X, and ignoring one's intrinsic interest in toy X. Guttentag and Longfellow then note Jones and Nisbett's (1972) finding that individuals overestimate environmental cues when they are finding causes for their own behavior (in the role of "actor"), but not in explaining the behavior of others (in the role of "observer"). Combining these assumptions (1) that overjustification is aided by a more salient environment, and (2) that actors experience a more salient ("engulfing") environment than do observers, it is possible to explain the phenomenon of children showing overjustification as at an earlier age than they show (other-directed) discounting. Stated simply, young children's discounting in self-directed attribution (overjustification effect) is accentuated by their perspective as actors; at the same time, their role as observers inhibits their discounting in other-directed attribution. In other words, young *actors'* attributional perspective tends to make them insensitive to motives in the face of external cues, while young *observers'* primary attributional error (overestimation of internal causes) retards their development of such a tendency.[3]

Admittedly, this is only a speculative application of the actor-observer hypothesis to a development phenomenon. However, it illustrates the potential for further integration of attributional and developmental approaches to social perception. It also illustrates a point that has been implicit throughout this chapters discussion of attribution of responsibility and causality. That is the general progress that has occurred in attributional-developmental research. It has progressed, first, toward methodological clarity and precision, as seen in recent studies of moral judgment. It has also progressed toward an investigation of the mechanisms that underlie developmental phenomena, such as the contrasting processes of cognitive development and the socialization of interpersonal judgment. Finally, it has progressed toward a developmental examination of more recent and sophisticated attributional phenomena, as exemplified by the discounting and overjustification effects.

Notes

[1]Apparently, English usage of the word "responsibility" has changed significantly over the last four centuries (*Oxford English Dictionary,* 1933). Similar to the legal concept of responsibility, the common language term originally described a mostly causal relationship (e.g., "effect B is responsible to cause A"). Subsequently, however, it was transformed into the more accountability-oriented term that is familiar today (e.g., "person A is responsible for effect B").

[2]Schultz et al. also studied the development of other attributional schemas, such as Kelley's (1972) augmentation principle. They found that the more complex schemas were slower to develop than the (relatively simple) schema of discounting alternative causes.

[3]A second factor that might mask children's use of discounting is experimenters' over-reliance on verbal reports. As Guttentag and Longfellow note, the overjustification literature uses behavioral observations, whereas discounting studies usually use verbal accounts as dependent variables. If young children's verbal ability lags behind their motor development, then this difference in children's mode of expression may explain some of the age difference between the discounting and overjustification literature.

Attribution of Freedom and Control

5

As Skinner (1971) suggests in his critique of the emphasis upon the concepts of freedom and control in psychological theory, people generally believe that their capacity to have freedom and control in their lives are integral to their well being and satisfaction. One frequently hears people make statements such as: "I had no other choice." "I felt overwhelmed by all the options." "I've got to get my act together." "I want to feel more in control in my relationships." Such statements reflect the centrality of the experience of freedom and control in our lives.

The proposition that people strive to be free and have control over themselves and their environments has played a major role in a number of theoretical statements (e.g., White's, 1959, notion of competence motivation; de Charms', 1968, origin-pawn analysis; Rotter's, 1966, internal-external control conception; and Brehm's, 1966, theory of psychological reactance). In these conceptions, people's attributions of freedom and control often were assumed to mediate other forms of behavior such as persistence at tasks and attitude change. However, in the 1970s, perceived freedom and control began to be examined in a more explicit fashion than in previous work.

At the outset, we should be clear in indicating that our concern is with *perceived* freedom and control. Whether or not people indeed have freedom and/ or control is a matter that has been debated for centuries in philosophy, but such debate need not restrict investigation of freedom and control as psychological experiences (see the volume edited by Perlmuter and Monty, 1979, for further discussion of this debate).

In this chapter, we will describe some of the extensive work concerned with the antecedents and consequences of attributed freedom and control.

Definitions

The attribution of freedom has been studied as an inference a person makes about self and about other. The attribution of control has been studied almost exclusively as an inference about self. Given the centrality of the concept of control in the field of psychology today, investigation of the attribution of control would appear to represent a meaningful direction for research in this area. Although the phenomena of attributed freedom and control sometimes have been treated, in effect, as virtually identical (de Charms, 1968), a theoretical distinction can be made. In a recent conceptual analysis of perceived freedom (which we will treat here as synonymous with "attributed freedom" and "perceived choice") and control, Harvey, Harris, and Lightner (1979) have suggested that perceived freedom may be thought of as an experience associated with the act of deciding upon the alternatives that we will seek. It is a feeling or attribution that accompanies a decision to engage in a certain action(s) as opposed to another or others. Harvey et al. also suggested that compared to perceived freedom, perceived control does not seem to be so wedded to the act of deciding. In this conception, people may feel free to choose from a wide range of actions but feel little ability to gain control over the course that they have chosen. Thus, perceived control is characterized as more of an ongoing experience than is perceived freedom.

Although this distinction linking perceived freedom to the act of deciding and perceived control to the outcome of the decision seems necessary, there is evidence that these experiences often are positively related and occur in almost a simultaneous manner. Harvey and Harris (1975) found a positive relationship ($r = .38$) between perceived choice in making a selection about which task to perform, and expectancy about control over behavior on the subsequent task. In this study, subjects made a selection about which type of visual stimulation they would be exposed to later in the experiment. Information about the types of stimulation was varied in order to manipulate their perceived positivity. Also, Harvey and Harris found evidence that in conditions producing high perceived choice (e.g., when decisions involved highly positive option), expectancy about feelings of internal control was higher than in conditions producing low perceived choice (e.g., when decisions involved negative options). Since the relationship between perceived choice and control was correlational in nature it is unclear from Harvey and Harris' study whether or not decisions involving positive options lead to high perceived choice *because they enhance expected control.* Such a possibility seems quite plausible, but it awaits further empirical inquiry.

Ascribed Responsibility

Perceived freedom and control have one central, similar role in the experience of people, namely: they both have strong implication for the ascription of responsibility for people's behavior and outcomes. If a person is seen as free in his/her decisions or in control of personal acts and outcomes, then that person typically is held responsible. And ascribed responsibility to a person usually varies as a direct function of the attribution of freedom or control to the person. Further, we ourselves probably operate in much the same way in making personal attributions that holds for making attributions to others; that is, if we think that we have freedom or control, we probably will think that we are (or were) responsible.

As was discussed by Harris in Chapter 4, perceived responsibility sometimes refers to the judgment of causality and sometimes to the imputation of moral blame. In research linking the concepts of perceived freedom, control, and responsibility, moral blame appears to represent more the goal of the ascribed responsibility than does imputed causality.

This goal for ascribed responsibility appears to be well illustrated in real life events involving conspiracies among groups of people arranged in echelons of power. The Watergate conspiracy is a good example. Those alleged conspirators lower in the hierarchy can claim that they are not responsible because those of higher rank made the decisions (i.e., they had choice what actions to take, including actions that might have led to better outcomes). They also may contend that superiors were in control of the ultimate outcome—if not the particular action sequence. Therefore, as this reasoning goes the persons in lower echelons should not be morally culpable for the outcomes of the activities.

A study by Harvey, Harris, and Barnes (1975) investigated perceived freedom and responsibility by actors and observers for a negative outcome event. In the procedure used by these investigators, actor-subjects were led to believe that they were administering shock to another person (actually an experimental accomplice) for incorrect answers on a learning task. Observer-subjects passively watched the procedure. The learner's emotional distress was revealed to the teacher and observer by a false feedback meter. It was found that the actor-teachers attributed less responsibility and freedom to themselves the more severe the distress exhibited by the learner. Presumably, actors made attributions in this fashion so as to maintain their self-esteem in the situation. Interestingly, observer-subjects showed a reversed pattern of attributions from that of actors. Observers attributed more responsibility and freedom to actors the more severe the learner's distress. For both actors and observers, attributions of freedom and responsibility were highly correlated ($rs > .50$). Harvey et al. argued that observers were using their attributions as a way of showing moral reprehension and possibly as a way of controlling future behavior by the actor that might lead to such distress on the part of others.

Freedom and Control and Attribution

The topics of freedom and control are central to attribution approaches because a basic tenet of most of these approaches is that people want to achieve order in their lives (e.g., Heider, 1958; Kelley, 1972b). How do people do that? The answer is by seeing themselves as free agents (de Charms, 1968) who have taken certain actions (and continue to do so) to achieve personal control. Kelley (1972b) addresses quite well the point about the importance of the quest for control when he says, "The purpose of causal analysis—the function it serves for the species and the individual is effective control. . . . Controllable factors will have a high salience as candidates for causal explanation. In cases of ambiguity or doubt, the causal analysis will be biased in its outcome toward controllable factors" (pp. 22–23).

Whether or not people see themselves or others as free is a critical matter in all of the early attributional analyses. In Jones and Davis' (1965) conception of correspondent inference, a person will not be seen as acting in line with a disposition if the action was not perceived to have been freely taken. Further, the intentionality component, so essential in the attribution of disposition to other, is theorized by Heider (1958) to derive from the perception that a person has freedom in the form of personal power (and the wish or want) to attain a certain goal via some action. In Kelley's (1967) ANOVA analysis, imputed freedom to the actor in taking an action must exist at least implicitly before the attributor engages in detailed consideration of what factors covaried with the action. The same logic holds for Bem's (1967, 1972) approach in which a perception of low freedom in taking an action results in little if any ascription of causality to self for the action or its consequences.

Determinants and Consequences of Attributed Freedom

In the next two sections, we will examine variables that have been found to affect attributed freedom and control and then consider some consequences of the feelings of freedom and control.

Determinants

Similarity in Attractiveness of Choice Options
This variable has been shown to affect one's feelings of freedom in the following manner. Consider a situation where Person A has played a game on a quiz show and won and has a choice between receiving a new Datsun 280Z and a Triumph TR7 and Person B who also has won on the show and has a choice between the Datsun 280Z and a Ford Pinto. Who will feel a greater state of freedom? Research indicates that Person A will feel more freedom because the options are rather similar, as compared to B's option (e.g., Harvey & Johnston, 1973; Jellison & Harvey, 1973). Person B's decision to take the more luxurious Datsun should be virtually a foregone conclusion and involve little feeling of freedom. The role of similarity of options in attributed freedom was first described by Mills (1970) who argued that there needs to be some uncertainty in the perceiver if freedom is to be felt. And it follows that similar options involve more uncertainty about

which one is best than do dissimilar options. Most of the early work on self-attributed freedom by Harvey and colleagues was predicated on Mills' perceptive articulation that uncertainty is a vital mediator of people's sense of freedom of choice.

Valence of Options

The previously described study by Harvey and Harris (1975) provided evidence for the rather common sense idea that more positive decision options are associated with a greater sense of freedom than are more negative options. As suggested above, positive options may convey a greater sense of freedom because they are associated with a greater feeling of personal control. This line of reasoning about the sense of control in influencing feelings of freedom may hold even more strongly if a person's options are both negative. For example, how much control and hence how much choice should a person feel who is faced with the decision of whether to die by firing squad or by cyanide gas.

Harvey and Harris argued that their findings offered support for an implication deriving from Skinner's argument in *Beyond Freedom and Dignity* (1971). By suggesting that people typically do not recognize the control that positive reinforcement exercises over behavior, Skinner implies that people would feel a greater expectancy of personal control over their behavior and would have a concomitant sense of greater freedom when confronted by positive options than when confronted by negative options. Harvey and Harris indeed found perceived control, similar to choice ratings, to be greater under more positive conditions. Thus, if teachers, parents, etc. want to motivate learners, these results and speculations suggest that giving learners a sense of freedom and control via positive decision options may be a fruitful practical step. Of course, to do so, one needs to know how positively or negatively the individual perceived various decision options.

Number of Options

Perhaps the most obvious determinant of perceived freedom is the number of options being entertained by the decision-maker. A straight-forward prediction might be that the more options the decision-maker has, the greater will be the attribution of freedom. Research by Harvey and Jellison (1974) provides some support for this prediction, with an important qualification. They found that a moderate number of choice options (six in the experimental task employed) led to a greater sense of freedom on the part of the decision-maker than did a small number (three) or a very large number (twelve).

Harvey and Jellison interpreted these data as suggesting that too many decision options are just as oppressive as too few in reducing people's perception of freedom. The individual's ability to eliminate options may be impaired when the task involves options that are not that distinctive from one another. All of the options were relatively similar in the choice situation studied by Harvey and Jellison see Kehoe, 1979, for an interesting discussion of this possible interpretation). This reasoning has some relevance to the central thesis in Toffler's (1970) book *Future Shock*. Toffler contends that in the modern world, people are besieged by alternatives. There are, for instance, numerous family and life style options available to the contemporary human being. Such an abundance of options (a state that might be thought to be conducive to high perceived freedom) may induce "future shock." Toffler suggests that the greater the number of options open to individuals, the greater will be their freedom. But when the number of options becomes too great, then freedom becomes "unfreedom," producing the negative states of bewilderment, frustration, and disorientation.

Consequences of a Decision

Do people sometimes attempt to absolve themselves of the responsibility for an ill-fated decision by reducing their retrospective perception of choice in making the decision? Much of the research on determinants of attributed freedom such as that reviewed above, has focused on perceptual-information determinants and has concerned relatively non-ego-involving decisions. But, it seems very likely that ego-defensive processes sometimes do influence self-attributions of choice. As noted in the earlier discussion of alleged conspirators, a common defense of persons accused of wrongdoing is to attribute little choice to themselves in becoming involved in the activities in question.

It seems clear that, based on research in this area, decision-makers may be motivated to present themselves as having had little freedom, or indeed may sincerely feel that way, in making the decisions (Harris & Harvey, 1975; Harvey, Harris, & Barnes, 1975) when their decisions have negative societal or personal consequences. A central issue unresolved by this work concerns our lack of knowledge about self-presentational strategies in either perceived freedom or perceived control phenomena. Do people who make decisions which have negative consequences present themselves as having little freedom simply as a presentation tactic to avoid the censure of others? Or do they *really believe* that they had little freedom in making the decision? Or do they present the options to themselves that way and then start to believe their presentation (see Bem, 1972; Weary Bradley, 1978)? These are some of the crucial questions whose answers must await further empirical work.

Personality of the Decision-Maker

One personality variable that appears to be meaningfully related to one's self-attribution of freedom is that of locus of control. The concept of locus of control (Rotter, 1966) provides a useful means for measuring individual differences of the extent to which reinforcement is viewed as a consequence of one's own behavior (internal locus of control) or a consequence of such forces as chance, fate, or powerful others (external locus of control). Intuitively, it would seem that people who have an internal orientation would perceive more freedom in making decisions than people who have an external orientation. In making decisions "internals," who are conceptualized as people who believe that their actions make a difference in determining what happens to them, may search for additional alternatives or seek ways of differentiating among seemingly similar options; such behaviors as these may be highly conducive to a sense of choice. In contrast, "externals," who are conceptualized as people who believe that they have little control over what happens to them, probably will not engage in these searching and differentiating actions and may have little sense of choice.

Research by Harvey, Barnes, Sperry, and Harris (1974) provided some evidence relevant to these ideas. These investigators, however, did not find a general tendency for internals to perceive more freedom than externals. The main results were that "internals" exhibited more differential reactions to the characteristics of the options in the choice situation than did "externals." "Internals" judged themselves as having more freedom than did "externals" when they selected from a set of positive options, and less when they selected from a set of negative options. Further, "internals" perceived greater freedom when options were close to one another in attractiveness than when they were either far apart or virtually identical, whereas external individuals exhibited much less sensitivity to the characteristics of the choice options (i.e., they did not perceive choice differentially when the options varied in attractiveness).

In sum, the variables of similarity in attractiveness of options, valence and number of options, consequences of a decision, and personality of the decision-maker have been found to influence systematically an individual's personal feelings of freedom. But, as we discuss below, other determinants have been investigated for attribution of freedom to others.

Other Determinants: Steiner's Conception

Although it is beyond the scope of our survey to discuss fully, an innovative program of work on perceived freedom has been carried out by Steiner (for reviews of this work, see Steiner, 1970, 1979). Most of Steiner's work embodies the theme that the perceiver evaluates the world in a highly rational way. In evaluating their state of freedom, individuals, it is theorized, take into account such factors as expenditure or costs in taking certain actions, amount of payoff perceived to accompany the various options of a decision, and the probability of attaining certain payoffs.

Steiner (1979) identifies three varieties of attributed freedom. These varieties are: (1) evaluative perceived choice or "good choice" which exists when a person feels that the value of choice options is at least as high as that of the appropriate alternatives that serve as a comparison for the decision at hand (e.g., the attributor may think, "Mr. Jones' vacation options are as good as anyone in his income bracket could possibly afford."); (2) discriminative perceived choice or "clear choice" which exists when a person can clearly discriminate which of a set of options is the best; and (3) autonomous perceived choice which exists when the options are quite similar, though not identical as in the previously described work by Harvey and Johnston (1973) and Jellison and Harvey (1973).

This interesting analysis of varieties of perceived freedom has not been probed very comprehensively thus far by Steiner and his associates. We should note that it overlaps with the previously described work by Harvey and his colleagues mainly as it focuses on the concept of autonomous perceived choice. There is, in Steiner's conception, little focus on the possibility that ego protective processes may operate in attributed freedom, as argued by Harris and Harvey (1975) and Harvey, Harris, and Barnes (1975). Also, Steiner (1979) suggests that actors and observers should be affected in much the same way by variables that influence perceived freedom. The previously described study by Harvey, Harris, and Barnes (1975), however, suggests that in a situation where moral culpability is in issue, actors and observers may diverge in their attributions of freedom, with actors concerned about maintaining their self-esteem and observers more concerned about control of the actor via ascription of blame.

As noted previously, most of Steiner's research on perceived freedom has concerned attribution of freedom to others. For example, in one provocative study, Davidson and Steiner (1971) proposed that the manner in which a reinforcing agent administers rewards and punishments is an important source of information concerning the agent's freedom. In their procedure, subjects were told that the investigation concerned the effects of teachers' behavior on students' performance. In a rigged drawing, the real subjects were always assigned the role of student; the other persons, who were experimental accomplices, were always assigned the role of teacher. The students' job was to try to solve anagrams which were created so that each subject would solve about the same number. The teachers were to observe the students and, if they desired, to reward the students' correct responses by giving them money; they could also punish wrong responses by taking money away from the students. The experimental manipulation involved the variability of the teachers' rewarding-punishing behavior. In one condition, teachers punished the students 100% of the time after incorrect responses and rewarded them 100% of the time after correct responses. In the other condition, teachers punished and rewarded 40% of the time. Following the task, subjects were asked to judge how free they considered the teachers to be in their rewarding-punishing behavior. As Davidson and Steiner had predicted, subjects who received 40% punishment and reward attributed much more freedom to the teachers than did those who were always punished and rewarded. Thus, these investigators suggest that variability in the behavior of a reinforcing agent (who could be a teacher, parent, or anyone) contributes to an attribution of freedom to the agent.

Acting in Line with Predisposition

Kruglanski and Cohen (1973) specified another important variable that affects attributed freedom to others. In this study, individuals received information about target persons' predispositions and behavior in a specific situation. The target people were described as being strongly in favor of cooperation between human beings; then they were described as having taken an action either consistent or inconsistent with that predisposition. It was found that greater freedom was attributed to the target persons when their behavior was consistent with their presumed predisposition than when it was consistent. This effect was explained on the basis of the assumption that freedom will be attributed to people who are personally responsible for their own behavior. Further, behavior that is consistent with individuals' predisposition on an issue should be more attributable to the individuals than to other factors. However, an important theoretical question derives from these data. We do not know what reasoning on the part of perceivers accompanies an act that is inconsistent with predisposition. Is it that the act was forced? Possibly, but situations may exist in which inconsistent acts are viewed as reflecting free will because they represent a departure from the constraints of an individual's socialized nature. The previously described study by Jones, Davis, and Gergen (1961) is suggestive of this possibility.

Consequences

Work on the consequences of attributed freedom has been pursued in a variety of theoretical domains and precedes in time research on determinants of attributed freedom. Our treatment of this literature will be brief, and the reader is referred to Steiner (1970) and Harvey and Smith (1977) for more extensive discussions.

Attributed Freedom in Dissonance and Reactance Work

Among the first researchers to examine perceived freedom systematically as a variable for investigation were the dissonance theorists Brehm, Cohen, and their associates. At the time of their early work on perceived freedom, these investigators were concerned mainly with Festinger's (1957) theory of cognitive dissonance. In the Brehm and Cohen (1962) version of cognitive dissonance theory, perceived freedom is considered to be necessary for the arousal of the averse motivational state of cognitive dissonance. This state presumably arises whenever an individual simultaneously holds two cognitions (attitudes, beliefs, etc.) that are inconsistent, and the existence of a dissonant state is assumed to give rise to attempts to reduce the dissonance. While Festinger (1957) did not explicitly theorize about how perceived freedom might be necessary for dissonance to occur, Brehm and Cohen and other dissonance theorists posited that an individual would not experience the dissonance dilemma unless he or she felt that there had been freedom in taking the act that led to the dilemma. The key element in the arousal of a state of dissonance is that of insufficient justification for carrying out an action. If a student cheats on an exam, dissonance should arise if the student feels that the cheating was not justified (e.g., the exam could have been easily handled through adequate preparation). Insufficient justification will not be felt if the student feels that the cheating was not a matter of personal volition. Perhaps all of the members of the student's social group cheated, thereby creating a perceived pressure to follow suit. Hence, if no personal volition is felt by the student, no feeling of insufficient justification should develop, nor should the state of dissonance arise.

Thus, perceived freedom is important in the process of dissonance arousal, because it has strong implication for the relationship between action consequence and responsibility. Research by Brehm and Cohen (1959), Collins and Hoyt (1972), and Calder, Ross, and Insko (1973) clearly shows that individuals will feel responsible for the consequences of a counter-attitudinal action (which was presumed to create dissonance) and engage in dissonance reduction processes when they feel they freely engaged in the action.

The central assumption in Brehm's (1966) theory of psychological reactance is that people cherish their behavioral freedoms and experience aversive arousal when they perceive that these freedoms have been eliminated or are being threatened. The perception that one is free, therefore, is a basic element in the arousal of reactance; unless an individual believes that he or she can "significantly control personal destiny p. 2," he or she cannot feel threatened (Wicklund, 1974). Once the person feels a sense of freedom, however, even the slightest threat to that freedom may arouse reactance (Andreoli, Worchel, & Folger, 1974). It is noteworthy that both quantitative and qualitative factors are involved in the experience of reactance. That is, the extent of one's ability to experience reactance depends on both the number of one's freedoms that are threatened and the felt importance of whatever freedom is seen to be in jeopardy. The former effect, relating the number of threatened freedoms to the amount of reactance aroused, was demonstrated by Sensenig and Brehm (1968) in a study of attitude change caused by attempted coercion. The latter effect, relating reactance to the importance of a threatened freedom, was shown by Worchel and Andreoli (1974) in a study of how reactance can be aroused by obligating behavior (e.g., personal favors).

In terms of the relevance of reactance processes for attributional phenomena, an interesting method of reactance reduction was shown by Worchel and Andreoli (1974). In this study, some subjects were given the opportunity to attribute a threat to their freedom to the environment rather than to a threatening person. For those who were offered this opportunity to attribute the threat to the environment, reactance-related behavior occurred to a significantly lesser degree than it did for those who were not given the opportunity. Presumably, this effect occurred because reactance was reduced since environmental attribution decreased the perception of threat to personal freedom

Finally, one encounters a puzzling matter in examining the reactance literature, namely: Although the perception of freedom presumably is integral to the operation of reactance, we know of no work in the area in which feelings of freedom have been probed as dependent variables or mediators between independent and dependent variables.

The Role of Attributed Freedom in Attribution Research

In almost every major theoretical statement of social attribution theory (e.g., Heider, 1958; Jones & Davis, 1965; Kelley, 1967), perceived freedom has played an important, if not crucial, role. Much of the emphasis on freedom has been in relation to the question of how we attribute dispositional qualities (such as attitudes to other people). Jones (1978) suggests that the theory of correspondent inference was based in large part on the idea that you can tell what a person is like if the person has choice in taking an action. In general, studies of the question of how dispositions are inferred have found that our perception of another's freedom is a key determinant of our perception of that person's attitudes (Jones, Davis, & Gergen, 1961; Jones & Harris, 1967; Steiner & Field, 1960). Some of this research has revealed that when an individual expresses a certain opinion with apparent freedom to do so or not to do so, others seem to be more confident in their attribution of a corresponding attitude to the individual. When an individual is seen as having little freedom in choosing which position to support, others have been found to pay relatively little attention to the behavior and base their attributions on other factors such as the individual's past behavior and attitudes.

Freedom not only affects our attribution of attitudes and dispositions, but it also affects our perception of the basic qualities of personal responsibility and causality for interpersonal events. As discussed by Heider (1958), the central factor in our attributing causality (and hence, responsibility) for an event to another person is our perception of the intentional nature of that person's behavior, and intentionality depends on attributed freedom from outside coercion. Thus our causal attributions to others depend on our perception of their freedom. As noted in the chapter on development of attribution, this point has been demonstrated by Harris (1977) who found that adults faced with a minor misfortune (the breakage of a chair) only attributed significant responsibility to the person involved in that misfortune when that person was perceived to act in a free, intentional manner.

Finally, Harvey, Harris, and Lightner (1979) have speculated about the role of attributed freedom in the attribution of mental illness. They suggest that the assessment of how much freedom and control the patient has is critical to the therapeutic endeavor. Concomitantly, however, Harvey et al. contend that the patient may get caught in a self-presentation bind in reporting his or her freedom and control. The patient wants professional help, but will such help derive from a perception on the part of the therapist that the patient is a relatively helpless pawn or a debilitated but promising organ of personal conditions (de Charms, 1968)? This bind appears to be especially true for the chronically ill patient who is kept in a state institution. Harvey et al. make this point in the following way:

"Often, almost any unusual behavior that they might exhibit could be seen as part of their illness (see, for example, the contrasting defense mechanisms of acting out and reaction formation); no matter how free and uncoerced a client's or patient's behavior may seem, therapists eventually may see it as determined and repetitious. As such, the behavior cannot be the basis of much new attribution about their improvement by observers, and therefore any previously labeled patient's characteristics would seem unusually fixed and unchanging. Thus, in the context of the concept of perceived freedom, we see an attributional reason for 'the stickiness' of both psychodiagnostic labels and psychodynamic clinical attributions" (p. 294).

Determinants and Consequences of Attributed Control

Determinants

There has been only a small amount of work directed toward examination of determinants of attributed control. As with work on determinants of attributed freedom, this research has emphasized an individual's personal sense of control, and there has been little work directed toward examining variables that may influence attribution of control to others.

One of the first studies to investigate determinants of self-attributed control was conducted by Wortman (1975). She predicted that individuals will feel control over an outcome if they cause the outcome and if they know before causing it what they hope to obtain. The procedure for this experiment involved asking subjects to rate a series of consumer items. They were told that the experimenter had a large supply of two of the items and that they would win one by a chance drawing. Each subject was instructed to take two marbles of different colors from a large bowl. One-third of the subjects were told that the experimenter would pick a marble to determine their prize, and they were also told beforehand which marble stood for which prize (experimenter caused-foreknowledge condition). One-third were told to select a marble to determine their prize, after being told which marble stood for which item (subject caused-foreknowledge condition. The remaining subjects were told to select a marble to determine their prize but were not told until after they had picked their marble which one stood for which prize (subject caused-no foreknowledge condition). An important aspect of the procedure was that neither the subject nor the experimenter was allowed to look in the bowl as the marble was being drawn. After subjects had won a prize based on their drawing of a marble, they rated their perceived control over the outcome.

Consistent with prediction, Wortman found that subjects who caused the outcome and had foreknowledge about it perceived themselves to have more control over the outcome than did subjects who did not cause it but had foreknowledge or subjects who caused it but did not have foreknowledge. Wortman's data indicate that the perception of personal causation and foreknowledge are directly related to feelings of control. She suggests that a central mediator of the effects of these variables on perceived control might be the effort persons perceive themselves as exerting on a task; the greater the perception of effort, the greater the feeling that one can really influence the outcome.

In another early examination of determinants of self-attributed control, Langer (1975) examined the idea that certain variables may induce a perception of control in situations where the outcomes are completely determined by chance (for example, lotteries). She found that perceived control was greater when subjects were (1) given a choice in selecting a lottery ticket than when they were not given a choice, (2) encouraged to become involved in a passive way by thinking about a lottery than when they were given no encouragement to become involved, and (3) encouraged to become familiar with a certain chance situation than when they were not encouraged to become familiar with it. According to Langer, these data suggest that variables such as choice, involvement, and familiarity, which are meaningful in helping people plan and develop strategies in nonchance situations, have a carry-over effect to chance situations in inducing an illusion of control. Langer's demonstration of variables affecting self-attribution of control is particularly impressive because success on the experimental tasks was unquestionably chance-determined. For this reason, Langer emphasizes that she was concerned with the "illusion of control."

Research concerned with the consequences of the psychology of control has not focused explicitly or closely on control as an attributional phenomenon. Thus, the brief review provided here only touches on this work and its implications for attributional analysis (see also Chapter 6 for discussion of control and learned helplessness). This work, however, suggests that individuals' thoughts and attributions may mediate the impact of stressful events on various types of behavior.

Consequences

In a series of important investigations on perceived control and predictability, Glass and Singer (1972) and their colleagues showed that whether a person is able to predict when aversive stimulation will occur has a pronounced effect on problem-solving ability and adaptation to stressful situations. The assumption that links this work on predictability to the experience of control is that the more predictable an aversive event is, the greater should be the individuals' ability to prepare their sensory apparatus so as to be less sensitive to the event or to schedule their actions so as not to be interrupted by the event. In several of the studies done by Glass and associates, subjects were to complete such simple tasks as number comparisons, addition, and letter finding. In a study by Glass, Singer, and Friedman (1969), these three tasks were performed by subjects under four conditions of noise distraction. The noise was a combination of the sounds of two people speaking Spanish, one person speaking Armenian, a mimeograph machine, a desk calculator, and a typewriter. The composite sound, a nondistinguishable roar, served as the aversive noise. In one experimental condition the subjects, who were college students, received the noise at 110 decibels (loud) for 9 seconds at the end of every minute of the session. In another condition, subjects received loud noise at random intervals and for random lengths of time. In two other conditions, subjects received either fixed or random noise but at a softer volume (56 decibels).

Glass and associates found that the initial bursts of noise were effective in distracting most subjects. As the session progressed, however, subjects adapted to the noise. They improved in performance on the simple tasks and exhibited less responsivity as assessed by physiological measurements. After this session, subjects were engaged in further tasks during which there was no noise or like interference. The results were very similar across tasks. It was found that subjects who experienced random noise exhibited poorer performance than did those who received fixed-interval performance. Loud noise at random intervals was associated with the highest level of impaired performance, whereas the softer noise at fixed intervals was associated with the best performance across tasks. Based on these results, it would appear that the consistency of noise has a marked impact on performance. Predictable noise does not have the same injurious effect on performance as does random, unpredictable noise.

The work by Glass and Singer and colleagues represents some of the best research on the consequences of perceived control. But it is unlikely that the subjects in these studies actually engaged in much deliberation about their state of control. Further, these investigators typically provided no data regarding the subjects' phenomenal experience of control. Thus, again there is only a moderately strong link between the consequences of perceived control and attributional activities engaged in by individuals involved in the stressful situations that were investigated.

Other findings relevant to the effects of attributed control also are indirectly relevant to attributional ideas, but a few bear brief mention. In the area of learning (paired-associate tasks), Perlmuter, Monty, & Kimble (1971) demonstrated that allowing subjects to think they were choosing materials they are going to learn enhanced their performance on various learning tasks. Subjects may have developed a greater sense of control for handling the tasks because of their sense of choice in selecting which task to learn.

In some rather dramatic research, Langer and Rodin (1976), Rodin and Langer (1977), and Schulz (1976) showed that certain manipulations that apparently gave institutionalized elderly patients a greater sense of control over their environment apparently led to more activity, more alertness, greater happiness, and greater health as compared to patients who did not receive these manipulations. The manipulations included giving patients small decisions to make and giving them various responsibilities (e.g., taking care of a plant). Langer and Rodin and Schulz suggested that their perceived control manipulations made subjects feel more competent. In further work, Langer and colleagues (e.g., Langer, 1979; Langer & Benevento, 1978) argued that the typical conditions surrounding institutionalized aged patients may lead to an erroneous inference of incompetence and self-induced dependence. To reinterpret the position of Langer and her associates slightly, conditions such as inferiority labels and passivity that are imposed on the patients may stimulate self-attribution process wherein the patient becomes convinced that he or she is incompetent and at the mercy of others' whims, or fate, or some other external agents (cf. Bem, 1972; Rotter, 1966).

In conclusion, this latter line of work with institutionalized patients seems to be moving closer to an analysis of the role of mediating cognitions such as attributions of control in the behavioral sequences. However, researchers in this area have not often probed directly individuals' thoughts or self-attributions. We as theorists and observers have too often inferred in a most indirect way what the subject-participants think. This neglected matter needs to be addressed in future work in this interesting area.

Theoretical Assimilation and Conclusions

In this chapter, we have reviewed theory and research concerned with people's inferences about their own and others' freedom and control. We have accorded the concepts of freedom and control leading roles in the unfolding of attributional phenomena. As Seligman and Miller (1979) suggest, people may opt for high perceived choice and control situations so as to enable them to match their internal states with external events, thereby making the overall outcome better. Such reasoning is quite compatible with our view of the import of these experiences in attributional analysis. Figure 5.1 presents the temporal framework for locating the variables of attributed freedom, control, and responsibility that was suggested in this chapter.

Essentially, Figure 5.1 presents a package of correlated perceptions. We do not wish to suggest certain necessary causal directions among these experiences. Causality may involve feedback loops where, for example, situations fostering the perception of choice enhance anticipated subsequent control; or, as suggested previously in the case of positive options, a sense of freedom may be increased by the perception that one will have control over the outcomes of options for action.

Figure 5.1

Proposed Temporal Framework for Occurrence Of Attributed Freedom, Control, and Responsibility

Time 1
Attributed Freedom Situation
(e.g., a student's perceived choice about how to make a good grade on a critical exam in college; options might include studying exceptionally long hours, hiring a tutor, and cheating via use of a social organization's files or the instructor's past exams)

Time 2
Act or Decision
(in the example, the student chooses how to respond to the challenge of the exam)

Time 3
Attributed Control Over Behavior or Outcome
(in the example, the control felt over performance during the exam—should correlate positively with sense of freedom in deciding on how to prepare for the exam)

Time 4
Attributed Responsibility For Performance
(in the example, it should be higher the more freedom and control the student is viewed as having had; the ascription of freedom no doubt may have an extremely negative consequence for the student when he/she is perceived to have cheated when other viable options existed)

This package may be extended somewhat by adding the feeling states of competence and satisfaction. Research by Jellison and Harvey (1973) and Harvey and Jellison (1974) revealed a moderate positive correlation between perceived choice and feelings of competence about making decisions. Also, Harvey and Jellison (1974) found a positive correlation between perceived choice in making a decision and satisfaction with the decision. The perceived choice-competence link needs a little more discussion. As Jellison and Harvey (1973) first noted, this relationship fits well with White's (1959) hypothesis that people are motivated to put themselves into situations in which they will learn about their competence. Jellison and Harvey suggested that high perceived choice situations maximize a person's ability to learn about his/her competence. If no choice is felt in the learning situation (e.g., regarding the way to solve a problem), then the person may learn less about personal competence regardless of the outcome of the decision involved in the learning act.

Thus, overall, it appears that several different psychological experiences relating to self-attribution, or more generally self-understanding, are interrelated in meaningful ways. But the reader may be asking at this point, are the self-attributions of freedom and control always positive, and do people always seek such states? Our answer has to be "probably not" to both inquiries. At a global, philosophical level, Fromm (1941) has suggested that Germans "escaped from freedom" in abdicating responsibility for reasoned rule of their country at the time of the emergence of the Third Reich. Perhaps Germans whose conduct at that time may be interpreted as surrendering responsibility were making a bargain, the reward for them being a stronger sense of strength associated with the unquestioned authority of Hitler. At a more personal level, there are several contemporary social psychological analyses which emphasize people's preference for an automatized approach—requiring little sense of freedom and control—to various kinds of tasks (see Langer, 1978, 1979). These lines of work, therefore, seriously challenge the "always" part of the contentions that the states of freedom and control are positive and sought by people.

Finally, there is one other intriguing line of work that has emerged regarding the feelings of depressed college students that bears mention in our attempt to put the assorted parts together in understanding attributed freedom and control. Alloy and Abramson (in press) report that depressed college students report more veridically the degree to which their behavior influences the outcome of environmental events as compared to non-depressed students, who report being in control when this feeling cannot be defended. Arnkoff and Mahoney (1979) make a similar observation regarding the more accurate perception of contingency by neurotics relative to nonneurotics.

How could these less than "normal" individuals be so perceptive in their inferences? We certainly cannot answer such a question with any clarity (and indeed the data are quite embryonic). But, if they are informative, perhaps such data suggest that "normal" people have a much greater tendency to delude themselves about their states of control (and freedom) than do "non-normals." In fact, maybe such an emphasis on the illusion of freedom and control often is a criterion of normality (cf. Skinner, 1971)? In this vein, Perlmuter and Monty (1979) masterfully analyze what the poet Shelley meant when he defined freedom as "that sweet bondage." They imply that such a contradiction may mean that to Shelley, freedom is the knowledge that indeed one is always in bondage to the variables and conditions that take their inexorable course in controlling our lives. Returning to the examples of work with depressives and neurotics, we may see such people as sometimes having achieved "that sweet bondage" by being stripped of the defenses and comforting illusions that are so much the daily armor of most of us.

Attributional Processes and the Development of Dysfunctional Behaviors

Within the last 15 years there has been an increasing tendency for theorists and researchers to acknowledge the importance of social-cognitive processes in the acquisition and maintenance of dysfunctional behaviors (e.g., Arnkoff & Mahoney, 1979; Bandura, 1977; Meichenbaum, 1977; Wortman & Brehm, 1975). Of particular interest has been the notion that cognitions about oneself may serve as mediators in the maintenance and modification of various behavior patterns. For example, response-outcome expectations (Seligman, 1975), efficacy expectations (Bandura, 1977), self-instructions (Meichenbaum, 1977), and self-statements (Ellis, 1962) have all been proposed as mechanisms involved in the pathogenesis, maintenance, and therapeutic treatment of a variety of behavioral disorders. Many of these cognitive explanations of dysfunctional behaviors involve attributional activities, and in this chapter we will examine empirical evidence relevant to the possible role of attributional processes in the development of clinically relevant target behaviors. In particular, we will examine attributional activities as they relate to Seligman's (e.g., Abramson, Seligman, & Teasdale, 1978) learned helplessness model of depression and to Storms and McCaul's (1976) model of the emotional exacerbation of dysfunctional behaviors.

An Attributional Analysis of Learned Helplessness and Depression

Depression is a disorder of the entire psycho-biological system (Burns & Beck, 1978) and generally involves somatic, emotional, and behavioral disturbances. Somatic symptoms of depression, for example, may include loss of sleep, appetite, or sexual desire. In addition, feelings of sadness, guilt, and despair, behavioral passivity, inactivity and social withdrawal are characteristic of depressive disorders. The following account was given by a clinically depressed female and illustrates many of the disturbances commonly reported by depressed individuals.

I can sum up my problems very easily. I'm a total failure in life. Nothing I do seems to work out. My married life is dull. My husband and I rarely do things together anymore—except argue. He just seems to be disinterested in me, and probably with good reason. Neither of my children are doing well in school. I know I should try to help them and try to be more supportive, but I just don't. I get mad and yell at them. I just don't have what it takes to be a good mother—or wife, I guess. Even my work is drudgery; my successes at work seem meaningless to me. I'm so tired. I don't have the energy to do much of anything. I really feel that my life is hopeless. I'd be better off dead. My family would be better off too if I were out of the picture.

It is clear from this account that the woman feels helpless and views most of her negative life outcomes as due to something about her. Her life, as she describes it, is a series of failures for which she is responsible.

Seligman and his associates have proposed that feelings of helplessness and attributions of self-blame interfere with the ability to respond adaptively in stressful situations and are important in the development of depression in humans. Before discussing Seligman's model of depression, however, we should point out that the model of learned helplessness was originally formulated on the basis of laboratory studies with infrahuman species. For this reason, it is necessary to discuss the basic experimental paradigm used in learned helplessness research with animals.

In most of Seligman's early studies of the learned helplessness phenomenon (Overmier & Seligman, 1967; Seligman & Maier, 1967; Seligman, Maier, & Geer, 1968), animals were exposed, during a "pre-treatment" phase, to controllable shocks, uncontrollable shocks, or no pre-treatment. They subsequently were placed in a shuttlebox containing two compartments separated by a barrier. In each experimental trial, a signal was presented for 10 seconds prior to the administration of an electrical shock. If the animal jumped the barrier during the signal period or after the shock began, the receipt of electrical shock could be avoided altogether or escaped. On the next experimental trial, the animal was required to jump back across the barrier in order to avoid or escape the signalled shock. In general, the results of studies using this general paradigm have indicated that relative to animals in the controllable shock or no pretreatment control conditions, animals who were pretreated with uncontrollable, inescapable shock failed during experimental trials to avoid or escape from the electrical shocks. Instead, these animals tolerated extreme amounts of shock passively.

This interference with escape-avoidance behaviors produced in animals by prior inescapable shock has been termed learned helplessness. Seligman (1973; 1975) has contended that the major causal factor in the development of learned helplessness is the organism's belief or expectancy that its responses will not influence the future probability of environmental outcomes (expectancy of response-outcome independence). According to Seligman, Maier and Solomon (1971):

S makes active responses during exposure to inescapable shocks. Because shock cannot be controlled, S learns that shock termination is independent of its behavior. S's incentive for initiating active instrumental responses during a shock is assumed to be partially produced by its having learned that the probability of shock termination will be increased by these responses. When this expectation is absent, the incentive for instrumental responding should be reduced. The presence of shock in the escape-avoidance training situation should then arouse the same expectation that was previously acquired during exposure to inescapable shocks: shock is uncontrollable. Therefore, the incentive for initiating and maintaining active instrumental responses in the training situation should be low. . . . In addition, learning that shock termination and responding are independent should interfere with the subsequent association of responding and shock termination. . . . More exposures to the new contingency should be required in order for S to learn that shock is controllable, because S has already learned that shock is uncontrollable. This is why we think preshocked dogs have difficulty acquiring escape and avoidance responding even after they once jump the barrier and terminate shock. (p. 369)

While a number of alternative interpretations have been offered as explanations for the learning deficits that result from exposure to uncontrollable outcomes (see Maier & Seligman, 1976, for a review), the learned helplessness interpretation has received the most attention and has been the most widely investigated.

Following the early helplessness experiments with animals, a number of researchers investigated the occurrence, nature, and parameters of learned helplessness in humans (Hiroto, 1974; Hiroto & Seligman, 1975; Klein, Fencil-Morse, & Seligman, 1976; Roth & Bootzin, 1974). Many of these studies of human helplessness attempted to reproduce the animal findings in humans (Abramson et al., 1978). For example, Hiroto (1974) assigned college students to a controllable noise, an uncontrollable noise, or a no noise training condition. In the test phase of the experiment, all subjects were tested for helplessness in an apparatus analogous to the shuttle box used in animal research. In the shuttle box, all subjects were informed that a loud noise would come on periodically but that they could terminate the noise by moving a lever from one side of the shuttle box to the other. Consistent with the results of animal helplessness experiments, Hiroto (1974) found that subjects who had previously been exposed to uncontrollable noise failed to escape the noise during the test phase, while controllable and no noise subjects readily learned the escape-avoidance response.

Similar performance deficits for subjects exposed to uncontrollable outcomes in the test phase of experiments concerned with human helplessness have been found by other investigators; it is important to note, however, that several studies have found increases in performance following learned helplessness training (e.g., Roth & Bootzin, 1974; Roth & Kubal, 1975). In an attempt to explain such "facilitation effects," Wortman & Brehm (1975) have suggested that when individuals who expect to have control over their outcomes are exposed to uncontrollable outcomes, they will experience psychological reactance (Brehm, 1966; 1972) and will exhibit increased motivation to exert control and improved performance. But through repeated exposure to uncontrollable outcomes, they will learn they cannot control their outcomes and will exhibit the performance deficits characteristic of learned helplessness.

The Learned Helplessness Model of Depression

In a major statement of his model of learned helplessness, Seligman (1975) has suggested that learned helplessness consists of three inter-related deficiencies: motivational, cognitive, and emotional. More specifically, Seligman has proposed that learned helplessness "(1) reduces the motivation to control the outcome; (2) interferes with learning that responding controls the outcome; (3) produces fear for as long as the subject is uncertain of the uncontrollability of the outcome, and then produces depression" (Seligman, 1975, p. 56). Noting the similarities between these deficits produced by exposure to uncontrollable outcomes and those characteristic of depression in humans, Seligman (1975) also has suggested that learned helplessness may be viewed as a model of naturally occurring depression in humans. That is, just as learned helplessness is produced by exposure to uncontrollable outcomes (expectancy of response-outcome independence), reactive depression may also be caused by feelings of loss of control over behavioral outcomes, and may be accompanied by cognitive, emotional, and motivational deficits similar to those that accompany states of learned helplessness (i.e., symptoms of passivity, negative cognitive set, and depressed affect). Accordingly, laboratory-induced helplessness should produce deficits parallel to those found in naturally occurring depression (Klein et al., 1976).

This learned helplessness model of depression has stimulated an impressive amount of research in the past 5 years. A study reported by Klein, Fencil-Morse, and Seligman (1976) is representative of this research. In their study, Klein et al. assigned depressed and non-depressed college students to one of five training sessions during which they received (a) solvable problems, (b) no problems, (c) unsolvable problems with no attribution of failure instructions, (d) unsolvable problems with internal attribution of failure instructions, and (e) unsolvable problems with external attribution of failure instructions. When subsequently tested on a series of anagrams, depressed students performed worse than non-depressed students, and students who had received unsolvable problems during the training session performed worse than students who had received solvable or no discrimination problems during the training session. Also, in accord with the learned helplessness model of depression, subjects who received unsolvable problems during the training phase showed performance deficits parallel to those exhibited by depressed students. Finally, Klein et al. (1976) found that when depressed students were led to attribute their failure to the difficulty of the problems rather than to their own lack of ability, performance improved significantly. Klein et al. (1976) concluded:

The learned helplessness model of depression is strongly supported by our results: Laboratory-induced helplessness produced deficits parallel to those found in naturally occurring depression. In addition, however, the learned helplessness model of depression needs an extra construct concerning attribution of helplessness to personal failure. . . . Because all the early helplessness studies were done with animals, the early theory did not need knotty constructs like attribution and personal adequacy. Now that helplessness can be studied in man and because helplessness has been proposed as a model for human depression, learned helplessness theory now needs to incorporate such mediational cognitions. (p. 516)

While the study by Klein et al. (1976) manipulated depressed individuals' causal ascriptions for their performance outcomes, a recent study by Kuiper (1978) examined depressives and non-depressives *typical* patterns of attributions for successful and unsuccessful outcomes. Specifically, in this study depressed and nondepressed college students performed a word association task and then received feedback indicating they had answered 20%, 55%, or 80% of the items correctly. Following task performance, students were asked to assign causal responsibility for their performance outcomes to effort, ability, task difficulty, and luck. The results indicated that nondepressives made internal attributions (ability, effort) for success and external attributions (task difficulty, luck) for failure. In accord with Klein et al.'s (1976) findings suggesting that learned helplessness is dependent upon exposure to failure *and* the attribution of helplessness to internal causes, Kuiper reported that depressives made internal attributions for failure. Contrary to expectations, depressives also made internal attributions for successful outcomes. In discussing these findings, Kuiper speculated that,

nondepressives' external attributions for failure may represent an effective strategy (i.e., the operation of a self-protective bias) for preventing the occurrence of depression. On the other hand, the depressive's tendency to make a personal attribution for failure may be a very ineffectual strategy for preventing the occurrence of depression. . . . For instance, it is possible that blaming oneself for failure may contribute to other features of depression, such as feelings of unworthiness, guilt, self-devaluation, and loss of self-esteem. (Kuiper, 1978, p. 243)

The results by Klein et al. (1976) and Kuiper (1978), then, suggest that for humans causal attributions following uncontrollable outcomes may mediate subsequent performance deficits. These results, however, also raise questions about the learned helplessness model of depression. For example, if depression results from a belief in response-outcome independence, why do individuals attribute causal responsibility for failure to themselves?

For a number of reasons including the failure to include mediational cognitions, such as causal attributions, in the original formulation of the learned helplessness model of depression, investigators of human helplessness and depression "have become disenchanted with the adequacy of theoretical constructs originating in animal helplessness [studies] . . ." (Abramson et al., 1978, p. 50). More specifically, Abramson et al. (1978) have noted that the original formulation of the learned helplessness model of depression suffers from four major inadequacies:

(a) Expectation of uncontrollability per se is not sufficient for depressed *affect* since there are many outcomes in life that are uncontrollable but do not sadden us. Rather, only those uncontrollable outcomes in which the estimated probability of the occurrence of a desired outcome is low or the estimated probability of the occurrence of an aversive outcome is high are sufficient for depressed affect. (b) Lowered self-esteem, as a symptom of the syndrome of depression, is not explained. (c) The tendency of depressed people to make internal attribution for failure is not explained. (d) Variations in generality, chronicity, and intensity of depression are not explained. (p. 65)

All but the first of these inadequacies have been addressed in a recent attributional reformulation of human helplessness by Abramson et al. (1978). It is to this reformulated model that we will now turn our attention.

Reformulated Model of Learned Helplessness

According to the reformulated model of helplessness, the individual first learns that certain outcomes are not contingent on his or her responses. The individual then makes an attribution regarding this non-contingency of responses and outcomes to stable-unstable, internal-external, and global-specific causes. This causal attribution determines the individual's subsequent expectation for future noncontingency, and the expectation, in turn, determines the helplessness symptoms that result (i.e., the generality and chronicity of helplessness deficits, and lowered self-esteem). The sequence of events that according to the reformulated model lead to symptoms of helplessness are illustrated in Figure 6.1.

To elucidate the role of attributions in the production of learned helplessness symptoms, Abramson et al. (1978), like other attribution theorists and researchers (e.g., Heider, 1958; Kelley, 1967; Weiner, 1974), have proposed that causal attributions can be classified along internal-external, and stable-unstable dimensions. The internal-external dimension differentiates those causes that are due

Figure 6.1

Sequence of events leading to helplessness symptoms. (Adapted from Abramson, Seligman & Teasdale, 1978)

Perceived ⟶ noncontingency	Attribution of ⟶ noncontingency to factors that are a. stable-unstable b. global-specific c. internal-external	Expectation ⟶ of future noncontingency	Helplessness Symptoms a. Chronic deficits b. general deficits c. lowered self-esteem

to some aspect of the person (e.g., ability or effort) and those that result from situational or environmental factors (e.g., task difficulty or luck). The stable-unstable dimension refers to factors that are long-lived and recurrent (e.g., ability or task difficulty) versus those that are short-lived and nonrecurrent (e.g., effort or luck). In their attributional reformulation of learned helplessness, Abramson et al. (1978) have argued that attributions may also be classified along a third dimension: global-specific. According to these authors, global factors occur across situations and affect a wide variety of outcomes, whereas specific factors are unique to the learned helplessness situation and do not generalize across situations.

What implications do attributions to internal-external, stable-unstable, and global-specific dimensions have for future expectations of noncontingency and symptoms of helplessness and depression? Abramson et al. (1978) have suggested that following a perception of non-contingency, attributions to internal factors lead to "personal helplessness" and depression (i.e., the person expects the outcome is not contingent on any response in his or her repertoire but that relevant others may have available the requisite response), while attributions to external factors lead to "universal helplessness" and depression (i.e., the person expects the outcome is not contingent on any response in his or her repertoire nor on any response in relevant others' repertoires). Moreover, attributions to internal factors are more likely to lead to self-esteem loss than attributions to external factors. In addition, attributions to stable factors should produce helplessness and depression deficits that are characterized by greater time-related characteristics than attributions to unstable factors. Finally, deficiencies attributed to global factors are more likely to generalize across situations than those attributed to specific factors.

Abramson et al. (1978) speculated that there may be a depressive attributional style. Specifically, these authors suggested that "the particular attribution that depressed people choose for failure is probably irrationally distorted toward global, stable, and internal factors and, for success, possibly toward specific, unstable, and external factors" (Abramson et al., 1978, p. 68).

Although not designed specifically to test predictions made by the attributional reformulation of the learned helplessness model of depression, the previously discussed studies reported by Klein et al. (1976) and Kuiper (1978) have examined attributions made by depressed and non-depressed college students for successful and unsuccessful outcomes. The results of these studies indicated that depressed students tended to make more internal attributions for unsuccessful outcomes than did non-depressed students.

These two studies, then, provide limited support for the reformulated model of helplessness depression. However, a recent study by Seligman, Abramson, Semmel, and VonBaeyer (1979) was designed specifically to assess whether the attributions of depressed people differ systematically from those of nondepressed people on *all three* attributional dimensions of internality, stability, and globality. To assess attributional style, Seligman et al. asked college students to name the one major cause of positive or negative outcomes of several hypothetical events and then to rate each cause for the degree of internality, stability, and globality. In addition, all subjects completed the short form of the Beck Depression Inventory (Beck, 1967) and a measure of transient depressive mood, the MAACL (Zuckerman & Lubin, 1965). Analyses of subjects' scores on the attributional style scale, the BDI, and the Multiple Affect Adjective Checklist (MAACL) indicated that relative to non-depressed students, depressed students attributed bad outcomes to internal, stable, and global factors. They also attributed good outcomes to unstable and external factors compared to non-depressed students.

The results of the study reported by Seligman et al. (1979) are consistent with the notion of a depressive attributional style and provide support for the attributional reformulation of learned helplessness and depression. It is important to note, however, that the college students in the present study were, at most, mildly depressed; consequently, there is a question "concerning the generality of the results of this study to populations of clinically depressed individuals" (Seligman et al., 1979, p. 247). It also will be necessary for future research to determine whether this attributional style is unique to depression or whether it is a feature of other psychopathologies. A final caution regarding the results of this study is in order: It is unclear whether the depressive attributional style found for positive and negative outcomes of the hypothetical situations used in this study will generalize to more behaviorally involving situations.

In summary, the attributional reformulation of the learned helplessness model of depression (Abramson et al., 1978) addresses many of the inadequacies inherent in the original formulation (Seligman, 1975). In addition, the studies reported by Klein et al. (1976), Kuiper (1978), and Seligman et al. (1979) taken together provide some support for the reformulated model as well as for the role of attributional processes in the development of helplessness and depression. However, several potentially important issues relevant to the study of learned helplessness and depression in humans have not been addressed by the reformulated model, and it is to these issues that we will turn briefly our attention.

Both the original and the reformulated model postulated that a perception of noncontingency between response and outcome was necessary for subsequent development of learned helplessness and depression. However, to date studies of learned helplessness and depression have employed only indirect and ambiguous measures of this perception of noncontingency. Rizley (1978) has noted that

One of the primary dependent variables used—changes in the expectation of success verbalized prior to each trial on an experimental task—is at best an ambiguous index of cognition or perception of response-reinforcement relations. One can clearly have a high expectation for reinforcement but a low expectancy for *control* over reinforcement, as when one feels "lucky" in a game of chance. Expectancy changes may also occur quite independently of changes in cognitions regarding controllability. (p. 33)

Examination of expectancy changes on experimental tasks, then, is not a direct way of testing the helplessness model. Future research will need to assess directly subjects' cognitions with respect to response-outcome relations.

A second issue not addressed by the reformulated model is that an expectation of uncontrollability per se does not seem to be sufficient to produce helplessness and depression. Specifically, Seligman (1975) originally suggested that learned helplessness will result from *any* noncontingent outcome, even positive reinforcement. Several investigators (Benson & Kennelly, 1976; Hiroto & Seligman, 1975; Roth & Bootzin, 1974; Roth & Kubal, 1975) have examined the occurrence of helplessness deficits following exposure to noncontingent positive outcomes. In general, the results of these studies are inconsistent, but the overall pattern of results suggests that noncontingent positive reinforcement does not produce helplessness (see review by Miller & Norman, 1979, for an overview). As Abramson et al. (1978) imply, both the contingency and the valence of the obtained outcome seem to determine the occurrence of helplessness.

The last major set of issues not addressed by the reformulated model concerns the difficulties involved in drawing parallels between learned helplessness and clinical depression. First, as Costello (1978) has pointed out, experimental evidence that exposure to uncontrollable outcomes causes subsequent behavioral deficits similar to those found in depression does not necessarily demonstrate that the same underlying process was responsible for experimentally and naturally-produced deficits. It is necessary to go beyond the simple identification of similar deficits. Second, Seligman has made no attempt to take the various types of depressive disorders into account. A considerable amount of research has been devoted to the investigation of the numerous clinical manifestations of, genetic and biological variables involved in, and the treatment response of the several subgroups of depression. The original and reformulated learned helplessness models of depression do not specify "to which subgroups the learned helplessness model is applicable, and how the concept of helplessness relates with other suspected etiologic factors associated with the various subtypes of depressive disorders" (Depue & Monroe, 1978, p. 4). Finally, it is important to note that most tests of the learned helplessness model of depression have used nonclinical undergraduate college students divided into depressed and nondepressed groups on the basis of self-administered rating scales. However, Costello (1978) and Depue and Monroe (1978) have noted that an elevated score on such scales can result from a number of factors unrelated to depression. In fact, these later authors (1978) have stated that "in the absence of other sources of history, psychosocial, and clinical data, a score on a rating scale is virtually uninterpretable with respect to diagnostic concerns" (p. 16). We should be most cautious in assuming, then, that relatively normal college students and more severely depressed clinical patients are similar. Clearly researchers interested in extending the learned helplessness model of depression to clinical populations will need to attend to these issues.

Attributional Processes and the Emotional Exacerbation of Dysfunctional Behaviors

In our preceding discussion of learned helplessness (Abramson et al., 1978; Seligman, 1975), we examined how attributional processes may produce behavioral deficits and depression. Storms and McCaul (1976) also have proposed that attributional activities may lead to severe psychological disturbances. Specifically, these authors have suggested that under certain conditions, attributions to self may increase symptomatic behavior by triggering anxiety. Consider, for example, the insomniac who upon retiring begins to wonder whether this will be another sleepless night. Suddenly, our insomniac notices that it's a little warm and the faucet in the bathroom is dripping. After tossing and turning for about an hour, it's still warm, the drip sounds like Niagara Falls, and it's getting lighter outside. Our insomniac gets more anxious and begins to wonder if her inability to sleep is really a symptom of some more serious psychological problem. It even occurs to our insomniac that she may be neurotic and need long-term psychotherapy.

This pattern of behavior is characteristic of a number of different emotional syndromes. In such a pattern, the individual becomes aware of an undesirable aspect of his or her own behavior, such as insomnia. From that individual's point of view, the behavior is a symptom of some underlying problem, a lack of control, a basic inadequacy. These negative self-attributions produce further anxiety that, in turn, exacerbates the original symptomatic behavior.

Storms and McCaul (1976) have formulated an attributional model to account for the emotional exacerbation of dysfunctional behaviors. These authors have proposed that a self-attribution of unwanted, dysfunctional behavior results in an increased emotional state of anxiety and that this anxiety may serve to increase the frequency or intensity of the dysfunctional behavior. Storms and McCaul noted that his exacerbation model should be applicable to three general categories of maladaptive behaviors.

First, behaviors which are comprised of specific physiological functions may be disrupted by anxiety. This category would include sleeping, sexual functioning, and perhaps certain motor tasks that require precise muscular movements. Second, behaviors which are habitual, well-learned responses may be increased by anxiety. This category may include various addictions, alcoholism, over-eating, and perhaps other typical emotional responses to stressful situations. Third, behaviors which require attention to appropriate cues may be affected by anxiety. This category would include driving and other perceptual-motor tasks, and test taking and other highly cognitive activities. (Storms & McCaul, 1976, p. 154)

In a test of their exacerbation model, Storms and McCaul (1975) examined the role of subjects' attributions about their speech disfluencies upon subsequent disfluency rates. More specifically, normal speaking subjects were asked to make two tape recordings of their speech. After subjects completed the first recording, the experimenter informed all subjects that they had displayed a very high number of disfluencies such as repetitions and stammers. Next, half of the subjects were told that their disfluency rate was a normal result of situational factors such as being in an experiment; the remaining subjects were told that their disfluency was a symptom of their own personal speech pattern and ability. All subjects then were asked to make the second tape under conditions of high or low situational stress (i.e., subjects were told that their second tape either would or would not be played with identifying information to a psychology class). Storms and McCaul (1975) predicted and found that self-attribution/high-stress subjects exhibited significantly greater increases in stammering than all other groups.

The results of this study provide support for the notion that the internalization of a negative self-attribution may lead to exacerbation of dysfunctional behavior. It is important to note, however, that the subjects in Storms and McCaul's (1975) test of their exacerbation model were normal speaking subjects; they had no real speech problem. In addition, while Storms and McCaul were able to produce temporarily an increase in stammering in the self-attribution/high-stress subjects, we cannot assume that the same underlying process is responsible for an experimentally-induced and a naturally occurring speech disorder. As also will be the case in future investigations of learned helplessness and depression, it will be necessary for researchers interested in the role of attributional activities in the emotional exacerbation of dysfunctional behaviors to go beyond the mere demonstration of experimentally-produced symptoms.

In this chapter, we have examined attributional processes as they relate to Seligman's (e.g., Abramson et al., 1978) learned helplessness model of depression and to Storms and McCaul's (1976) model of the emotional exacerbation of dysfunctional behaviors. Both models propose that causal attributions influence an individual's cognitive, behavioral, and emotional reactions to stressful life events. This emphasis on social-cognitive processes has stimulated a considerable amount of research on the development and maintenance of dysfunctional behaviors and has highlighted the necessity of placing psychopathology within its social context. However, researchers will need to be mindful of the many problems involved in drawing parallels between naturally occurring and experimental analogues of maladaptive behavior patterns.

Attributional Processes, Treatment of Maladaptive Behaviors, and the Maintenance of Behavior Change

7

In the preceding chapter, we reviewed several current areas of research that illustrate the potential importance of attributional processes in the etiology and maintenance of various dysfunctional behavior patterns. This research in social and cognitive factors involved in the development and maintenance of maladaptive behaviors has also been accompanied by an increased interest in the incorporation of attribution principles to treatment procedures (e.g., Kopel & Arkowitz, 1975; Ross, Rodin, & Lombardo, 1969; Valins & Nisbett, 1971). In an early paper, Valins and Nisbett (1971) attempted to describe how social psychological research on attribution processes may be relevant to the area of clinical practice. Since the appearance of this paper a number of researchers have investigated the application of attributional principles to the treatment of clinically important problem behaviors. In this chapter, we will examine both social psychological and clinical research relevant to two major forms of attributional treatments of various maladaptive behaviors: misattribution and reattribution training therapies. We also will examine the empirical evidence regarding the possible relationship between a patient's attributions about his or her treatment improvements and the maintenance of his or her behavioral changes.

Aversive Emotional States and Misattribution Treatment Intervention

Misattribution of Source of Arousal

More often than not clients initiate or are referred for psychotherapeutic treatment because of distressing emotional states which are interfering with their daily functioning. It is not uncommon, for example, for individuals to seek treatment for anxiety that interferes with their sleeping, their performance on exams, or their ability to interact with strangers. Before considering how attribution processes may play a role in the treatment of such distressing emotional experiences, it is necessary to consider the possible role of causal attribution in the production of emotions.

As described in chapter 2, Schachter (1964) has proposed a theory of emotion which posits that both perceptible physiological arousal and labeling of this arousal in accord with situational or cognitive factors are necessary for the subjective experience of emotional stress. An attributional analysis of Schachter's theory suggests that diffuse physiological arousal motivates the individual to make causal attributions about the source of his or her autonomic arousal and that these causal attributions in turn provide the individual with cognitive labels (e.g., fear or anger) for the arousal state (Ross, Rodin, & Zimbardo, 1969; Valins & Nisbett, 1971). According to this analysis, then, physiological arousal attributed to an emotionally relevant source should result in emotional behavior. The specific nature of this behavior would, of course, depend upon the nature of the cognitive label attached to the arousal state. However, physiological arousal attributed to a nonemotional source should not result in emotional behavior.

This attributional analysis of Schachter's (1964) emotion theory has stimulated a considerable amount of research. Much of this research has attempted to demonstrate that undesirable emotional behaviors (in particular, defensive behaviors) may be reduced by leading individuals to misattribute their heightened autonomic arousal to nonemotional sources.

In an early study designed to test this misattribution of arousal notion, Nisbett and Schachter (1966) attempted to persuade subjects that physiological arousal accompanying fear of electrical shocks was actually produced by a non-emotional source. Specifically, these investigators told subjects they would receive either a series of mild electrical shocks (low-fear condition) or a series of painful electrical shocks (high-fear condition). Prior to receiving the shocks, all subjects were given a placebo pill and a description of physiological reactions alleged to be side-effects of the drug. For one half of the subjects the description of side-effects included physiological symptoms characteristic of fear, while for the remaining subjects the description of side-effects included physiological symptoms irrelevant to fear.

As predicted, subjects in the low-fear condition who were led to believe their physiological arousal was due to the drug (i.e., those subjects who were given descriptions of fear relevant side-effects) found the shocks less painful and tolerated higher shock intensities than did low-fear condition subjects who were led correctly to attribute their arousal to the electrical shocks. Moreover, a postexperimental questionnaire indicated that the attribution manipulation was successful with low-fear subjects. In contrast to subjects in the low-fear conditions, Nisbett and Schachter (1966) reported that high-fear subjects did not differ in their reports of pain or tolerances of electrical shock as a function of the attribution manipulation. Further, the postexperimental questionnaire revealed that the attribution manipulation was not successful for subjects in the high-fear conditions. That is, most of these subjects attributed their heightened physiological arousal to the electrical shocks, regardless of the drug or shock attribution instructions. The investigators had expected that their attribution of arousal manipulation would not be effective for high-fear subjects since the anticipation of painful electrical shocks would be too plausible an explanation for their arousal.

While Nisbett and Schachter's study demonstrated that subjects could be verbally persuaded to misattribute their arousal to a non-emotional source and subsequently to display a reduction in emotional (i.e., defensive) behavior, it also suggested that misattribution might be possible only "within the limits of plausibility." Specifically, the results of this study indicate that misattribution of arousal might not be possible when individuals have a salient and plausible explanation (e.g., painful electrical shocks) for their extreme emotional responses.

Recognizing that this limitation could greatly limit the potential application of misattribution procedures in clinical settings, Ross, Rodin, and Zimbardo (1969) conducted a study designed to serve "as an experimental analogue to plausible therapeutic techniques" (p. 279). Ross et al. reasoned that for highly fearful individuals, misattribution procedures might be more effective if the correlation, or causal connection, between the emotionally relevant source and physiological arousal were obscured. In this study, subjects were told that the purpose of the experiment was to determine the effects of distracting noise on task performance. The task required subjects to learn to assemble two puzzles. Subjects were told that the solution of one of the puzzles would lead to a monetary reward, while the solution of the other puzzle would allow them to avoid an electrical shock. In fact, both puzzles were insoluble. Next, all subjects were informed that the noise to which they would be exposed during task perofrmance might have side effects. Half the subjects were led to believe that they would experience side effects which correspond to the usual physiological correlates of fear (e.g., palpitations). The remaining subjects were led to believe that they would experience side effects which are not usually associated with fear but which could be associated with noise bombardment (e.g., ringing sensation in the ears). These experimental instructions were intended to induce subjects to attribute their physiological arousal state (produced by the anticipation of receiving painful electrical shocks) either to the threat of shock or to a cognitively neutral source (i.e., noise bombardment), and they consistently were presented contiguous with the onset of arousal symptoms. Finally, subjects were presented with the two puzzles and allowed to spend as much of the available test period working on each puzzle as they wished.

Ross et al. reasoned that the greater fear of shock would be reflected by more time spent on the shock-avoidance puzzle. Moreover, higher levels of fear should be exhibited by shock attribution subjects who were not given the opportunity to misattribute their physiological arousal to the cognitively neutral source. In accord with predictions, the results of this study indicated that shock attribution subjects spent significantly more time attempting to solve the shock-avoidance puzzle than did noise attribution subjects.

Ross, Rodin, and Zimbardo's (1969) study, then, demonstrated that even for highly fearful individuals, avoidance behaviors could be reduced through misattribution techniques. The generalizability to clinical settings of the results of this study, as well as those reported by Nisbett and Schachter (1966), is questionable, however, since neither of these studies used clinically relevant target behaviors nor clinical populations.

Clinical Applications of Misattribution of Source of Arousal Techniques

A first attempt at testing the implications of misattribution therapy techniques for a clinically important problem was provided by Storms and Nisbett (1970). Before describing the Storms and Nisbett investigation, let us consider a real world example that may illuminate different aspects of the misattribution process depicted by these investigators. Suppose a student becomes extremely anxious before taking exams and consults a clinician about this problem. One possible treatment might be some type of tranquilizing drug. Another possibility might be to give the student an extremely mild tranquilizer or a placebo but to tell the student that the drug will lead to a very high level of relaxation. The question arises: During the next exam, will the student, who may feel some anxiety, think about the clinician's description of the effects of the drug and become *less* anxious? Or will the student think that the presumably strong drug was unable to relieve this anxiety and therefore, become *more* anxious (i.e., will the student think that if he or she is anxious despite the medication, then his or her anxiety must be very severe)?

In an attempt to answer such questions, Storms and Nisbett asked insomniacs to take a placebo pill a few minutes before going to bed. Subjects were told either that the pill would produce physiological symptoms characteristic of arousal (e.g., alertness, palpitation, high body temperature) or that the pill would produce physiological symptoms characteristic of relaxation (e.g., relaxation, lowered heart rate, decreased body temperature). The authors reasoned, "to the extent that an insomniac goes to bed in a state of autonomic arousal and associates that arousal with cognitions that are emotionally toned, he (or she) should become more emotional and have greater difficulty getting to sleep" (p. 320). However, if an insomniac is led to attribute part of his or her arousal at bedtime to a drug, he or she should experience less emotionality and, consequently, get to sleep sooner. In accord with these predictions, Storms and Nisbett (1970) found that insomniacs anticipating drug effects characteristic of arousal reported getting to sleep more quickly on nights they took the pills. Also as predicted, insomniacs expecting drug effects characteristic of relaxation reported getting to sleep less quickly on nights they took the pills, presumably because they assumed that their emotional responses must have been extremely intense to have counteracted the effects of the relaxation pill.

Storms and Nisbett's (1979) study, then, has obvious clinical relevance. It suggests that if a client's problems are exacerbated by anxiety over symptoms, providing the client with a non-emotional source for his or her physiological arousal will reduce maladaptive emotional behavior. However promising Storms and Nisbett's results appear for clinical applications of misattribution techniques, it is important to note that the results obtained by these investigators have been difficult to replicate. For example, studies reported by Kellogg and Baron (1975) and Bootzin, Herman, and Nicassio (1976) found direct suggestion, or placebo, effects rather than the reverse placebo effect obtained by Storms and Nisbett. That is, in both of these studies insomniacs given drug-arousal instructions identical to those used by Storms and Nisbett (1970) reported an increase in time to fall asleep. Because of these failures to replicate the results reported by Storms and Nisbett and because of the sole reliance of self-report measures of latency to fall asleep in the Storms and Nisbett (1970), Kellogg and Baron (1975) and Bootzin et al. (1976) studies, the clinical potential of misattribution techniques with insomniac clients remains largely undetermined.

In a conceptual replication of Storms and Nisbett's (1970) design, Singerman, Borkovec, and Baron (1976) examined the effects of misattribution of arousal manipulations on another clinically relevant problem, speech anxiety. These investigators asked highly and moderately anxious speech phobic subjects to present two speeches. During the presentation of the speech, subjects were exposed to meaningless noise in a manner similar to the procedures employed by Ross et al. (1969). Subjects were told either that the noise bombardment was known to increase physiological arousal (arousal condition) or that it was known to suppress or eliminate physiological arousal (sedation condition). In addition, all subjects were informed that their speeches would be videotaped for later evaluation and that an observer would be rating their performances during the speech presentations.

The results reported by Singerman et al. (1976) failed to replicate the misattribution effects found by Storms and Nisbett (1970), Ross et al. (1969), and Nisbett and Schachter (1966). Consistent with the findings reported by Kellogg and Baron (1975) and Bootzin et al. (1976), the results of self-report and behavioral measures of anxiety indicated direct placebo or suggestion effects; when noise was present, arousal subjects exhibited slightly and nonsignificantly more anxiety than did sedation subjects. Singerman et al. (1976) noted that the failure to replicate misattribution of arousal effects was likely due to the failure of their attribution manipulation. Most subjects attributed their heightened physiological reactions to anxiety about public speaking regardless of the arousal or sedation instructions.

It is important to note that this failure of the attribution manipulation in the Singerman et al. (1976) study is entirely consistent with Schachter's (1964) theoretical statement and with experimental results reported by Nisbett and Schachter (1966). Schachter stated, "given a state of physiological arousal for which an individual has no immediate explanation, he will 'label' this state and describe his feelings in terms of the cognitions available to him" (p. 53). However, if the individual has a ready explanation for his or her arousal, then he or she will be unlikely to search for alternative causal explanations. In the Singerman et al. (1976) study, it seems reasonable to argue that subjects had an immediate and salient causal explanation for their arousal. That is, the salience of anxiety caused by speech presentations may have been exaggerated by the experimenters' emphases on (a) taping subjects' speeches for later evaluation, and (b) observers' ratings of subjects' performances. It is not surprising, then, that subjects labeled their arousal as caused by the speech situation.

From this examination of misattribution of arousal studies using both non-clinical target behaviors (Nisbett & Schachter, 1966; Ross et al., 1969) and clinically relevant problems (Bootzin et al., 1976; Kellogg & Baron, 1975; Singerman et al., 1976; Storms & Nisbett, 1970), what conclusions can be drawn regarding the therapeutic potential of misattribution of arousal techniques? Studies by Nisbett and Schachter (1966) and Singerman et al. (1976) suggest that it may be difficult to manipulate attributions about the source of arousal with certain clinical problems, such as phobias, where the emotional response is clearly associated with a salient explanation. With such clinical cases, the more extreme and/or chronic the emotional response, the more difficult it probably would be to manipulate the client's belief about the source of arousal. Often, however, the source of a client's distress may not be apparent or may become more ambiguous during the course of treatment. Consider, for example, the coed who initiates treatment because she is experiencing considerable anxiety associated with reduction of cigarette smoking. In this case, the source of the coed's anxiety may seem obvious. However, during the course of treatment, she also discloses that she is anxious about graduating from college, about not having a job, and about her boyfriend interviewing for jobs in another state. In this example, the source of the coed's arousal becomes less apparent. As a result, the clinician may be able to effect a reduction in her level of anxiety by persuading her to attribute her arousal to some relatively neutral source. In psychologically ambiguous conditions, then, misattribution techniques may be effective in reducing arousal regardless of the intensity or chronicity (chronical character) of the emotional state.

Several authors have dismissed the therapeutic potential of misattribution of arousal techniques (e.g., Bandura, 1977; Bootzin et al., 1976, Singerman et al., 1976). Such a position, however, would seem to be premature. Misattribution of arousal studies that have used clinically relevant target behaviors suffer from methodological problems (e.g., sole reliance on self-report measures of behavioral change, failure of attribution manipulations) and, consequently, leave any questions regarding the clinical usefulness of misattribution of source of arousal procedures unanswered.

Before examining another variant of misattribution therapy, it is important to note that Leventhal and his associates (Calvert-Boyanowsky, 1975; Levanthal, 1974; Leventhal, Brown, Shacham, & Engquist, 1979) have argued that the reduction of avoidance behavior typically found in misattribution studies might have been due not to the emotional relabeling of bodily states, but to the mere presentation of veridical arousal information. More specifically, these authors have noted that in all of the misattribution studies they have considered, a major difference between arousal and sedation subjects has been the receipt of veridical arousal information by the former and the receipt of nonveridical arousal information by the latter. Thus, any observed reductions in emotional behavior by the arousal subjects might have resulted from the congruence between their expectations of physiological reactions and their actual experience. Whether decreases in emotionality are due to causal inferences regarding the source of arousal or to congruence between expectations and observation of actual arousal symptoms will be determined by future research. However, it is clear that veridical preparatory information about physiological reactions does affect emotional behaviors.

Misattribution of Degree of Arousal

According to Schachter's (1964) theory of emotions, both perceptible physiological arousal and labeling of this arousal in accord with situational or cognitive factors is necessary for the subjective experience of emotional states. In the preceding section, we examined studies that investigated the possibility of manipulating individuals' beliefs about the source of their heightened physiological arousal. The possibility that actual autonomic arousal may not be necessary for the production of emotional responses as long as individuals *believe* they are aroused has been investigated in a series of studies conducted by Valins and his associates (Valins, 1966; Valins & Ray, 1967).

In the studies of greatest clinical interest, Valins and Ray (1967) suggested that the reduction of avoidant behaviors produced by systematic desensitization might be dependent upon the manipulation of cognitions about internal reactions to the phobic stimulus. These investigators had unselected subjects (study I) randomly view ten slides of snakes and ten slides of the word "shock." In addition, presentations of the shock slides were followed by single administrations of mild electrical shocks. While viewing the slides, experimental subjects heard what they believed to be their heart rate increase in response to the shock but not to the snake slides. Control subjects heard the same sounds as the experimental subjects but were told that they were meaningless sounds. Valins and Ray reasoned that to the extent experimental subjects believe they are no longer affected by the phobic stimulus (i.e., slides of snakes), they also will believe they are no longer afraid of snakes and will exhibit more approach behavior when subsequently exposed to a life snake. The obtained results supported this hypothesis; experimental subjects approached and held a live snake more often than did control subjects. It is important to note, however, that this effect was statistically singificant only after subjects who had previously touched a snake were excluded from the analyses.

Valins and Ray (1967) conducted a second study in order to examine whether manipulation of cognitions regarding internal responses would affect avoidance behaviors in subjects whose fear of snakes was more extreme. Specifically, in this second study Valins and Ray recruited subjects who reported on a preexperimental questionnaire that they were afraid of snakes. The procedure for this second study was identical to that used in the first with two exceptions. First, subjects viewed through a one-way mirror a live snake in a glass cage instead of the slides of snakes. Second, in place of the conventional behavioral avoidance task used in the first study (and in most studies of systematic desensitization), Valins and Ray (1967) used the amount of money required to induce subjects to touch a snake as a measure of snake-avoidance. This task was used because Valins and Ray felt the conventional task might be too frightening for subjects whose fear of snakes was relatively intense. Consistent with the results of the first study, the experimental subjects, led to believe that they were not aroused following exposure to the caged snake, required less pressure (i.e., less money) to touch the live snake than did control subjects.

Valins and Ray's (1967) studies of the effects of "cognitive desensitization," or the misattribution of the level of arousal, suggest that persuading a client to believe that he or she is no longer afraid of a phobic stimulus is sufficient to reduce avoidance behaviors. A number of investigators, however, have criticized the therapy analogue procedure employed by Valins and Ray in their studies. More specifically, the results reported by Valins and Ray have been called into question because (a) a relatively weak behavioral posttest was used in study II (Bandura, 1969); (b) a behavioral pretest of fear associated with snakes was not employed, and such pretests typically eliminate a large number of subjects who report fear on a screening questionnaire (Gaupp, Stern, & Galbraith, 1972; Kent, Wilson, & Nelson, 1972; Sushinsky & Bootzin, 1970); (c) the obtained behavioral effects might have been due to differential attention paid by experimental subjects to their supposed heart-beats (Stern, Botto, & Herrick, 1972); (d) an aversion-relief model (i.e., a procedure whereby two stimuli are randomly presented, and one of the stimuli is followed by an electrical shock while the other is followed by no aversive consequence and thus takes on reinforcing properties) could account for the obtained group differences in avoidance behavior (Gaupp et al., 1972), and (e) the results of physiological measures of arousal were not reported (Gaupp et al., 1972; Stern et al., 1972). More importantly, the results reported by Valins and Ray (1967) have been difficult to replicate.

A recent experiment by Conger, Conger, and Brehm (1976) attempted to address several of the issues noted above. These authors argued that failures to replicate the results of Valins and Ray (1967) may have occurred for two possible reasons:

Subjects in the replication studies were generally more fearful than those in the original study, and the use of a behavior pretest may have mitigated the effect of false heart-rate feedback (Conger et al., 1976, p. 135.)

In their study, Conger et al., examined the proposition that fear level may be a moderator of the effect of false heart-rate feedback. Specifically, subjects whose fear of snakes was relatively high or low were assigned to noise or false heart-rate feedback conditions. The experimental procedure used in the Conger et al. study was nearly identical to that employed by Valins and Ray (1967). In addition to investigating the effects of fear level, these investigators varied the contiguity between shock and snake slides in order to provide a direct test of the aversion-relief explanation of Valins and Ray's results. As predicted, low-fear subjects in the feedback condition exhibited more approach behavior toward a live snake than low-fear subjects in the noise condition. However, high-fear subjects showed no effects on the behavioral posttest as a function of feedback versus noise conditions. Conger et al. (1976) also found no support for the aversion-relief explanation of the effects of false heart-rate feedback on avoidance behavior.

Conger et al. (1976), then, demonstrated that fear level is a critical factor in the replication of Valins and Ray's (1967) results; that is, reduction in avoidance behaviors via manipulation of cognitions about internal reactions was evident only for subjects whose fear of snakes was relatively low. The finding that behavioral effects resulting from misattribution of degree of physiological arousal are difficult to obtain with high-fear subjects is consistent with Schachter's (1964) theory of emotion and with the conclusions drawn earlier regarding misattribution of source of arousal studies (e.g., Nisbett & Schachter, 1966). Some degree of psychological ambiguity concerning either the source of heightened arousal or the level of physiological arousal seems to be necessary in order to manipulate attributions and the labeling of emotional states. Thus, when a highly fearful individual experiences a salient and intense internal reaction in response to a fear-relevant stimulus, it would probably be difficult to modify his or her interpretation about the level of the internal response.

Such a conclusion is clearly disappointing in terms of the clinical potential of misattribution of degree of arousal procedures. The level of fear (or other distressing emotional states) experienced by many clients is likely to make the use of such procedures difficult. Moreover, ambiguity with respect to the source of arousal is more likely to exist or to be more easily created in clinical populations than ambiguity concerning the degree of internal reactions.

Attribution Retraining Treatment Interventions

In the preceding sections of this chapter, we examined studies relevant to the possibility of a misattribution therapy, an intervention whereby the adoption of a new attribution for arousal symptoms might result in the lessening of undesirable effects of those symptoms. In this section, we will examine another variant of attributional approaches to behavior change, attribution retraining. This attributional approach to behavior change is concerned not with altering attributions regarding physiological arousal but, rather, with altering an individual's "attributional style" in response to specific aversive events.

Before examining studies relevant to attribution retraining interventions, it is necessary to note that the area of behavior change has recently seen a proliferation of treatment strategies (Bandura, 1977) such as rational-emotive therapy (Ellis, 1962) and cognitive-behavior modification (e.g., Meichenbaum, 1977), that emphasize the importance of cognitive processes as mediators of behavior change. Moreover, many of these cognitively-based treatment interventions examine aspects of a client's cognitions or "internal dialogues" other than self-attributions (e.g., self-appraisal, expectancy, competence, self-reinforcement). Several of these treatment approaches appear to have considerable clinical potential and have stimulated a good deal of research. However, here we will focus only on studies designed to investigate the possibility that attributional styles may be modified and that such modifications may result in more adaptive behavioral patterns.

As noted in the preceding chapter, the phenomenon of learned helplessness (i.e., the perception that responses and outcomes are independent) has been implicated in the etiology and maintenance of several maladaptive behavior patterns (e.g., Abramson, Seligman, & Teasdale, 1978, Dweck & Goetz, 1978). For example, Dweck and Repucci (1973) examined the role of children's attributions to learned helplessness in achievement settings. These investigators found that children most likely to give up as compared to those who persisted when confronted with failure (a) took less responsibility for their achievement outcomes and (b) to the extent they did assume responsibility, tended to attribute success and failure to ability rather than to effort. In addition, helpless children showed greater performance decrements following failure than did perseverance children. Dweck and Repucci (1973) suggested that attribution retraining may be a promising treatment intervention for helpless children.

Subsequently, Dweck (1975) conducted a study to determine whether altering helpless children's attributions for failure would result in changes in their maladaptive responses to failure on a problem-solving task. In this study, twelve children who experienced extreme reactions to failure were required to perform sets of math problems for twenty-five daily sessions. In addition, the children were exposed to one of two training programs; one group of children received successes only, while the other group received successes and failures. In the former group (success only condition), successes were attributed by the experimenter to the subjects' responses. In the latter group (attribution retraining condition), failures were attributed by the experimenter to lack of effort. The author predicted that children taught to attribute failure to lack of effort would demonstrate increased perseverance and improved performance when compared to children who received only success experiences. The results supported these predictions; following training, children in the success only treatment continued to show severe deterioration in performance after failure, while children in the attribution retraining treatment maintained or improved their performance.

Miller, Brickman, and Bolen (1975) also have provided evidence regarding the relative usefulness of attribution retraining treatments in maladaptive achievement behaviors. In one of their studies, Miller et al., attempted to modify second-grade students' math-related self-esteem and performances on tests of math skill. These authors found that repeatedly attributing either the ability or the motivation to do well in mathematics resulted in significantly greater increases in math self-esteem and math test scores as compared to persuasive or no-treatment control procedures. While students who received verbal praise and extrinsic reinforcement produced a similar pattern to that of the attribution treatment conditions, they did exhibit a lesser degree of improvement. The results of a delayed post-test administered two weeks after treatment had terminated indicated attribution treatments also were superior to persuasion and reinforcement interventions in maintaining the students' improvements. Miller et al. argued that the attribution treatments were more effective than treatments based on persuasion because they produced less counterarguing, resistance, and reactance.

The studies by Dweck (1975) and Miller and his associates are promising in terms of the clinical potential of attribution retraining treatment interventions. However, the application of such interventions to chronic and often debilitating behavior patterns in adults needs to be carefully examined in future research.

Attributional Processes and the Maintenance of Behavior Change

That causal attributions may be implicit in treatment interventions is forcefully illustrated in the following interview excerpts presented by Whalen and Henker (1976) in their exmination of attitudinal and cognitive correlates of Ritalin administration. These comments of an eleven-year-old demonstrate how positive behavior change can be attributed to medication and, in addition, how misbehavior can be attributed to nonmedication:

> Child: Well, sometimes I go in the bedroom and start crying because I need it, you know. And then my mother will come in and ask me what's wrong, and I'll say, "Daddy won't let me take my pill." She'll say, "Come on down here—I'll give it to you." So, I'll go down and she'll give it to me."
>
> Interviewer: So, sometimes you can really tell that you need it.
>
> Child: Yeah. [Pause] Sometimes I get mad at my dog and if I start getting mad at my dog, my Mother will say, "Go take your pill." I'll say, "Ah—O.K.," and I'll go downstairs and take it and then I come back upstairs and start saying "I'm sorry" to my dog.
>
> [Later]
>
> Child: At school two boys that know karate are gonna teach me how to do it. If I don't take my pill I'll start doing it on them.

Several other authors also have acknowledged the possible attributions that may follow from various treatment procedures and have stressed the importance of such attributions in maintaining positive behavioral change (e.g., Bandura, 1977; Brehm, 1976; Meichenbaum, 1977; Valins & Nisbett, 1971). For example, Bandura, Jeffrey, and Gajdos (1975) have stated:

Attributional processes may similarly delimit gains from success experiences. When disinhibition is facilitated by extensive supports, people may ascribe their success to external aids rather than to their own restored capabilities. Generalization decrements are more likely to occur if bold performances are attributed to special situational arrangements, rather than to regained personal competence (p. 142).

An early study by Davison and Valins (1969) examined the possibility that behavior change attributed to oneself would persist or be maintained to a greater degree than behavior change attributed to an external agent such as a drug. Subjects in Davison and Valins' "experimental analogue of drug therapy" (a) received a series of shocks and indicated their pain thresholds and shock tolerances, (b) ingested a pill (actually a placebo), (c) repeated the series of shocks with shock intensities surreptitiously halved by the experimenter, and (d) again indicated their pain thresholds and tolerances. Because the experimenter had reduced the shock intensities, all subjects presumably were led to believe that the drug had improved their threshold performances. Next, half of the subjects were told they had been given a placebo, while the other half were given no such information. In a third series of shock, it was found that subjects who attributed their behavior change to themselves (i.e., those who believed they had ingested a placebo) tolerated more shock and perceived the shocks as less painful than did subjects who attributed their behavior change to the drug. These results suggest that if an inividual attributes positive behavior change to medications, and consequently does not feel responsible for the behavioral improvement, he or she is unlikely to maintain the change once medication is stopped. However, if an individual attributes positive behavioral changes to himself or herself, such changes are more likely to persevere.

A study by Davison, Tsujimoto, and Glaros (1973) also examined the generalization of treatment gains as a function of attributions about the causes of such gains. However, this study may be more relevant to clinical settings than the Davison and Valins (1969) study since Davison et al. were concerned with a clinically relevant target behavior, insomnia. In this study, insomniacs participated in a week-long treatment program consisting of pharmacological elements (administration of a mild, but effective sleeping aid) and psychological procedures (self-produced relaxation and scheduling of evening activities prior to going to bed). Following treatment, half the subjects were told that they had received an optimal dosage of the sleeping aid, while the others were told they had received a dosage that was too weak to have been responsible for any improvement.

Following this attributional manipulation, all subjects were asked to discontinue the drug but to continue the relaxation and scheduling procedures for an additional week.

The results indicated that both optimal and minimal dosage groups showed equivalent and significant treatment effects; i.e., subjects in both conditions reported shorter latencies to sleep in the treatment than in the baseline weeks. Moreover, greater maintenance of treatment gain during the posttreatment week was demonstrated by subjects who could not attribute their improvement to the drug. These results offer support for the notion that behavioral changes believed to be due to an external agent, like a drug, generalize less to the posttreatment situation than changes believed to be due to one's own effort. However, the posttreatment period employed by Davison et al. (1973) was very short. It is possible that the generalization effects dissipated over time. Only one study, to our knowledge, has examined the association between self-attributions for behavioral change and long-term maintenance. In this study of the long-term reduction of cigarette smoking, Colletti and Kopel (1979) reported that superior maintenance of treatment gains was associated with a greater degree of self-attribution at a one-year follow-up, regardless of the specific maintenance strategy employed.

The studies by Davison et al. (1973) and Colletti and Kopel (1979) appear to provide meaningful support for the role of self-attributions as predictors of maintenance of behavior change. Also, several authors (e.g., Bandura, 1977; Brehm, 1976; Valins & Nisbett, 1971) have noted that induction of desired attributions for treatment gains need not involve deceptive manipulations. For example, internal attributions for behavioral improvements may be induced by gradually reducing and eliminating external aids once a client is performing the desired behaviors.

In conclusion, attribution therapies have been enjoying increasing popularity in the modification of maladaptive behavior patterns and in the maintenance of treatment gains. While the evidence indicates that misattribution and attribution retraining treatment interventions may be useful therapeutic procedures, it also suggests that under certain conditions misattribution regarding the source and level of physiological arousal may be difficult to achieve. In particular, research indicates that it may be difficult to manipulate attributions about the level and/ or source of arousal with certain clinical problems, such as phobias, where the emotional response is clearly associated with a salient explanation. Future research will need to assess for which clinical disorders attribution therapies are effective. In addition, investigators will need to assess the *clinical* utility of research findings relevant to attributional processes and the treatment of maladaptive behaviors. While treatment gains may be statistically significant, the clinical significance of such gains will need to be determined before actual treatment programs based upon attributional principles are developed.

3

The Future

Emerging Directions and Issues in Attribution Theory and Research

8

In this chapter, we will present a final commentary on what we see as some of the major contemporary issues and directions in attribution work. To some extent, this commentary reflects themes presented in earlier chapters, but it is intended to be more directly relevant to the future of attribution work.

Inadequate Work on Basic Attribution Theories and Concepts

We implied in chapter 1, and Shaver (in press) has discussed in some detail, the fact that present work in the attribution area reflects only minimal concern with *basic psychological processes* analyzed by pioneering theorists such as Heider, Jones, and Kelley. While recent analyses have called into question basic assumptions underlying attributional approaches to social perception and phenomenal causality (e.g., discussion in chapter 3 of work by Nisbett and colleagues, Abelson, Langer, and colleagues, and the ethnogenic school), in no substantial way have these critical analyses been concerned with refining central concepts discussed in chapters 1 and 2. For example, major ideas such as discounting, causal schemata, non-common effects, and divergent perspectives have received inadequate theoretical and empirical attention in the mid- to late 1970s. And despite recent theoretical work such as Jones and McGillis' (1976) reformulation of correspondent inference theory and Shaver's (in press) treatment of aspects of causal schemata and covariation, it seems unlikely that there will be an era of renewed work on basic processes in causal inference in the near future. As we will elaborate below, new currents of work that involve integration and application appear likely to predominate in the near future.

In a recent review, Kelley and Michela (1980) addressed this concern about work on basic process questions in the future when they said,

"In most respects, we feel, the problems of the field are those of psychology in general, reflecting too few researchers spread thinly over many problems. Each question has received far less attention, in terms of number of paradigms and replications, than its definitive and undoubtedly complex answer requires. Conceptually . . . the theories are piecemeal and greatly in need of synthesis. Here again the problems are those of psychology in general, which lacks conceptual frameworks for meshing cognitive, motivational, and behavioral factors" (p. 494).

Integrations of Attribution and Other Approaches

On the positive side, however, there now are underway major new directions of work on attribution. One major direction involves the integration of attributional analyses with research and theory of other areas of social psychology and other disciplines. This integrative approach emphasizes interactions among various systems within the perceiver (cognitive, affective, motivational, and behavioral) and interactions between such intrapersonal systems and more molar systems (e.g., social contexts). In the section below, we will discuss integrative work that appears to have much potential as a future direction in the field.

Attribution and Self-Presentation

A major future direction of attribution theory and research in the next decade probably will be an emphasis upon self-presentational and attributional activities. For example, there is considerable evidence that individuals attempt the strategic control of the responses of others by establishing a particular identity and that this identity is established in part through individuals' verbal descriptions of the causes of their behaviors. For example, if a presenter attributes unsuccessful task performances to internal factors (e.g., lack of ability or effort), the presenter may be attempting to project to others an appearance of modesty.

Recently, Weary and Arkin (in press) have proposed a model that integrates self-presentational and attributional processes. Specifically, these authors have proposed that the process of establishing an identity in an interaction episode can be broken down into five basic components: (a) the strategically controlled behavior of the presenter; (b) the presenter's perception of his or her own behavior and the context in which the behavior occurred; (c) the actual reactions of the audience in response to the presenter's behavior; (d) the presenter's attributions regarding the responses of the audience; and (e) the presenter's self-concept. Since Weary and Arkin are concerned with the possibility that self-attributions of causality may be viewed as strategic self-presentations, the first component of this model (i.e., the intentionally controlled behavior of the presenter) would include the presenter's judgments, or descriptions, of causal influence. The model also includes five major classes of variables that may be expected to influence the nature of the causal judgments strategically presented to others: (a) aspects of the task and attributional context; (b) the presenter's interaction goals; (c) social norms; (d) individual difference variables; and (e) characteristics of the audience (real or imagined). This model of the attributional self-presentation process is illustrated in Figure 8.1.

Figure 8.1

Proposed Model of the Attributional Self-Presentation Process. (Adapted from Weary and Arkin, in press

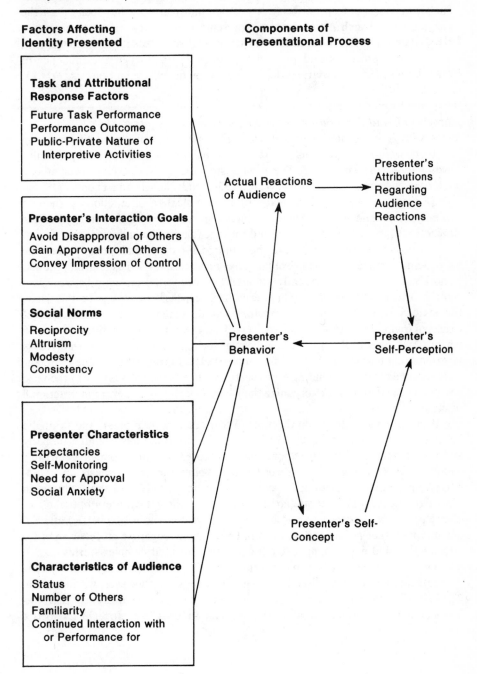

Factors Affecting Identity Presented

Task and Attributional Response Factors
Future Task Performance
Performance Outcome
Public-Private Nature of Interpretive Activities

Presenter's Interaction Goals
Avoid Disappproval of Others
Gain Approval from Others
Convey Impression of Control

Social Norms
Reciprocity
Altruism
Modesty
Consistency

Presenter Characteristics
Expectancies
Self-Monitoring
Need for Approval
Social Anxiety

Characteristics of Audience
Status
Number of Others
Familiarity
Continued Interaction with or Performance for

Components of Presentational Process

Actual Reactions of Audience

Presenter's Attributions Regarding Audience Reactions

Presenter's Behavior

Presenter's Self-Perception

Presenter's Self-Concept

While generally supportive of the model illustrated in Figure 8.1, Weary and Arkin (in press) noted that the majority of research designed to provide an integration of the self-presentations conceptual framework with attribution research has concerned the conditions that affect one's description of the causes of one's behavioral outcomes. Relatively little empirical work has focused on the consequences of such attributional self-presentations. Such work will be necessary for a more complete understanding of the role of self-presentational concerns in attributional processes and for a more adequate analysis of the influence of attributional self-presentations on the regulation of self-evaluation.

Attribution and Symbolic Interaction

An emphasis on how people structure their phenomenologies to give meaning to their worlds is the focus of several sociological approaches, in particular symbolic interaction theory. The most systematic early statement of symbolic interactionism was presented by Mead (1934) and Thomas and Thomas (1928). They theorized about the primacy of communicative interaction in shaping minds, selves, and society. Mead, in particular, emphasized that things become objects as they take on meanings, and that meanings—including the meaning of self as object to itself—are established interpersonally. He also emphasized the social and personal significance of language processes, the self as a social product, and social behavior as critically affected by an internal dialectic between two phases of the self, impulse and internalized responses of others. In this view, behavior is dependent upon a symbolized world; symbols attached to features of the environment (physical and social) carry meanings in the form of shared behavioral expectations that develop out of social interaction. Furthermore, it is reasoned that when people enter an interactive situation, they define it by applying symbols to it (including other participants and themselves). They then use the resulting definitions to organize their behavior through relevant interactional cues.

Recently, both attribution theorists (Weary & Arkin, in press) and symbolic interaction theorists (Stryker, 1977; Stryker & Gottlieb) have pointed to many of the similarities of the two approaches, as represented in particular by Mead's and Heider's writings. These theorists have pointed to the emphasis upon subjective experience, including the symbol usage and definition of the situation, in both approaches. Further similarities include the theoretical presumption of interdependence of cognitions and behavior (see related discussion below) and the assumption that people engage in complex symbolic-cognitive processes in order to simplify and make manageable (i.e., to control) their complex worlds.

This convergence of two major approaches in psychology and sociology represents an exciting new direction in the field. It is not, however, without limitations. For example, Stryker and Gottlieb (in press) have argued that the conception of self often found in attributional analysis (e.g., Jones & Nisbett's

1972 divergent perspectives hypothesis) is quite minimal when compared to the extensive analysis of the self in symbolic interactional work. It is conceivable that on both theoretical and empirical grounds, attributional work such as that being carried out by Weary and Arkin (in press) will not only redress this difference, but also provide a foundation for integrative research on concepts drawn from the two approaches.

Attribution and Social Behavior

For many years, a number of scholars have encouraged work specifically designed to probe the relationship between attribution and behavior (e.g., Heider, 1958; Kelley, 1972b). To date, however, few investigators have actually attempted to examine empirically how attribution is related to behavior during an ongoing social interaction. With regard to research that has addressed social perception-behavior linkages, the work of Snyder and associates (e.g., Synder & Gangestad, in press; Snyder & Swann, 1978) represents perhaps the most systematic exploration of such relationships. These investigators have studied how people often form hypotheses about others and then engage in actions that confirm the hypotheses they had formed. In an early study in this program (Snyder, Tanke, & Berscheid, 1977), men interacting via intercom with women whom they perceived to be physically attractive or unattractive elicited different kinds of responses from the two kinds of women. More specifically, it was found that the male who thought the telephonic partner to be attractive expected her to be sociable, poised, and socially adept, and, importantly, he himself was more sociable, bold, and attractive (as judged by independent raters) in his interaction with her. The self-confirmation cycle was further demonstrated such that the women (who were naive subjects) showed behavior consistent with the male's expectations—again, as judged by raters.

Additional evidence about the process of self-confirmatory hypothesis-testing was provided by Snyder and Swann (1978). They found that perceivers who interacted with persons previously labeled as hostile displayed greater hostility in their own behavior when compared to perceivers who interacted with persons previously labeled as nonhostile. Moreover, Snyder and Swann found that if the labeled person was encouraged to attribute the behavior in question to self, that behavior was exhibited in subsequent interaction with an innocent, previously uninvolved person. Snyder and Gangestad (in press) provide a comprehensive review of this line of research on self-confirmation.

A recently commenced research program bears some similarity to the work of Snyder and his colleagues, but it places greater emphasis upon the mediational role of attribution in channeling social behavior within an interaction episode. In a representative study, Yarkin, Harvey, and Bloxom (in press) investigated the relationships among cognitive sets about a person, attribution about that person, and subsequent interaction with the person. Subjects were given either positive, negative, or no set information about the emotional health of a stimulus person prior to observing the person in a videotaped interaction. Then subjects received a free-response attribution measure or a distraction task. Finally, all subjects engaged in an actual interaction (that was surreptitiously assessed by judges) with the stimulus person.

A principal finding emerging from the Yarkin et al. work was that subjects receiving the healthy or positive set information reported more positively-valenced attributions and displayed more positive behavioral responses toward the stimulus person when compared to subjects receiving unhealthy or negative and no set information. Additionally, Yarkin et al. provided evidence showing in part that dispositional attributional activity about the stimulus person mediated the subsequent behavior (i.e., was associated with pronounced increases in positive behavior or negative behavior, depending upon condition).

These investigators argued that prior sets may channel both attributions and behavior in a fashion that is conducive to the perceiver's/interactor's interest in understanding other and having some control over the subsequent interaction. Presumably, the affectively-laden sets used in their study initiated distinctive positive or approach and negative or avoidance responses toward the stimulus person; given the stimulus person's alleged psychological state of mind and the fact that only one brief interaction was scheduled to occur, both positive and negative orientations may be seen as serving the control motive. Finally, Yarkin et al. suggested that their investigation may provide a methodological foundation for study of the rich, natural complexity of sequence of set, attribution, and behavior.

Attribution and Social Cognition

A final integrative direction to be discussed is the social cognition or information-processing approach to attributional phenomena. Recently, much work representing this approach has been published (e.g., see Wyer & Carlston, 1979; Hastie, Ostrom, Ebbesen, Wyer, Hamilton, & Carlston, 1980). Our coverage, therefore, will be brief.

Researchers who have adopted the social cognition approach have argued that knowledge of such molecular, basic cognitive processes as encoding, retrieval, information integration, and response selection contribute substantially to an understanding of attributional phenomena. They have suggested that their basic cognitive process orientation provides a broader conceptual framework for locating attribution.

As an illustration of the social cognition approach, Wyer (in press) argued that information about the social world is encoded and organized with reference to schemata or configurations associated with features of people and events acquired through real world experience (note this argument bears some similarity to Kelley's, 1972, depiction of causal schemata). Suppose a perceiver receives information about another person's antisocial behavior. The information may be verbal or nonverbal and may include descriptions of not only the actors' behavior, but also his or her appearance, traits, and social role and characteristics of the audience and situation in which the behavior occurs. Wyer (in press) suggested that the encoding or "interpretation" of this type of information may occur in stages. First, subsets of information (e.g., traits of the actor) may be interpreted in terms of pre-existing schemata that are drawn from long-term memory. If a sufficient number of features of this information are also contained in the schema within which it is compared, the schema are considered applicable, and the information is encoded in terms of it. But if the perceiver has no particular reason for using the information (e.g., does not have to interact with the stimulus person), then the processing may end.

Adequate conceptualization and testing of such intricate cognitive processing is far from complete. Nevertheless, this social cognition approach is a feasible direction for contemporary work on attribution. It stands in sharp contrast to the more molar directions for integration discussed above. These integrative approaches may be seen as complementing one another fairly well, and not differing so much on the basis of fundamental assumptions as they do on the basis of level of analysis.

Applications

The application of attribution concepts toward understanding real world phenomena represents another major direction for research in the field. This direction is symbolized by a recent volume edited by Frieze, Bar-Tal, and Carroll (1979) that reports theory and research on the application of attribution principles to social problems.

Application to Clinical and Counseling Psychology

In chapters 6 and 7, we already have discussed the expanding segment of work concerned with psychopathology and attribution. This general area of work is burgeoning, and a few other strands deserve mention here. For example, the related topic of the attributional aspect of deviance has been studied by Koeske and Koeske (1975). They offered data to support the hypothesis that adolescent deviance under conditions of high perceived adult power promotes a perception of identity and a feeling of internal locus of control. More specifically, Koeske and Koeske found that high school students rated by teachers as "deviant," but not those rated as "conformant," showed greater internality (on a modified Rotter I–E scale) under conditions in which the students had rated their teachers as powerful. Of course, the extent to which this study can be generalized is questionable, since in no clearly determined way can the "deviant" students be conceived as deviant in the societal context of deviance (e.g., they were not carefully drawn from a population of adolescents who had been in trouble with the law).

Two other related programs of work reveal the breadth of application to clinical and counseling psychology. As mentioned in chapter 7, Whalen and Henker (1976) have discussed various attributional implications of using drugs to improve the behavior of hyperactive children. They noted that drug administration promotes an external (i.e., organic) attribution for the problem which the child and parents find comfortable. They concluded, however, that such a consoling causal inference may interfere with the acceptance of treatment programs that rely on teaching self-control strategies. In another vein, counseling procedures have been discussed from an attributional perspective (Strong, 1978). For example, Strong suggested, "A key to successful psychotherapy is to lead clients to identify a cause of their problems that they can control. The cause must be something the person does in situations, which he could do differently, such as the way he perceives events, his thoughts, beliefs, or attitudes about and in the events, or his actions to others in events. These personal causes are amenable to the person's will and effort and, in turn, affect other events such as other people's behavior. Changes of these personal causes can create vast changes in the person's intrapsychic and interpersonal environment" (p. 114). A similar point has been made by Bandura (1977).

Application to Education

In chapter 2, we mentioned the relevance of work by Weiner and his associates for educational practice. As was noted in that chapter, Dweck's (1975) attribution retraining technique is illustrative of how attributions of effort may be integrally involved in students' attempts to master learning tasks and actual mastery of them. A detailed analysis of attribution ideas relevant to education is provided by Weiner (1979).

Application to Close Relationships

Another area of application concerns how people engaged in intimate relationships make attributions about major events in the course of their association and about the causes for conflict, separation, and divorce. Weiss (1975), a sociologist, made a very informative study of marital separation which has strong attributional implications. He conducted in-depth interviews with separated persons living in the Boston area. Most of the respondents had been separated for a relatively brief period of time. The data were essentially case-history reports. Both males and females were interviewed, but no attempt was made to compare responses of ex-partners. Participants came mainly from the organization called Parents Without Partners.

Weiss (1975) postulated that people involved in the act of separation develop an account of what happened and why:

The account is of major psychological importance to the separated, not only because it settles the issue of who was responsible for what, but also because it imposes on the confused marital events that preceded the separation a plot structure with a beginning, middle, and end and so organizes the events into a conceptually manageable unity. Once understood in this way, the events can be dealt with. They can be seen as past, over, and external to the individual's present self. Those who cannot construct accounts sometimes feel that their perplexity keeps them from detaching themselves from the distressing experiences. They may say, "If only I knew what happened, if only I could understand why" (pp. 14–15).

In further discussion of the accounts that people often develop in the act of separation, Weiss implies that divergent explanations are quite pervasive: "None of the events significant to him appeared in her account, nor were any of the events significant for her included in his account" (p. 15). Weiss noted that these divergent accounts usually are selected by individuals from a bewilderingly complex range of events preceding and surrounding a separation, and he noted that accounts, as well as the perceived and actual events upon which they are based, may constantly be reviewed in an obsessive-like ritual performed by the individual in trying to make sense out of what has happened. The accounts represent themes centering on such matters as infidelity and betrayal, a desire for new things in life, perceived overreactions to activities (such as various degrees of extramarital intimacy), and freedom from constraints imposed by the partner.

Two other studies dealing more specifically with attributions about conflict in close relationships have been carried out by Orvis, Kelley, and Butler (1976) and Harvey, Wells, and Alvarez (1978). In both studies, it was found that in reacting to questions about the bases of disagreement and conflict, individuals tended to make attributions of blame to their partner. Orvis characterized this pattern as follows:

"The relationship requires that he/she be concerned about justification and exoneration. Similarly, the partner is no mere observer. Having been affected negatively by the behavior, the partner is concerned about its meaning, about redress or retribution, and about preventing its recurrence" (p. 364).

An interesting conclusion deriving from these studies is that in *continuing* relationships, attributions of causality serve a communicative role in defining, emphasizing, and acknowledging the basic understanding within the relationship about the conditions under which various behaviors may and may not occur. Furthermore, it was concluded that extensive attributional work occurs in close relationships primarily when things are going bad—when there is conflict and talk of termination. Although persons may at the beginning of such times genuinely seek the explanations for the conflict, their tendency appears to be to move soon to a phase in which attributions are communicated in order to express justification or criticism.

Concluding Points on Application

In conclusion, we have touched on only a few areas of application in this discussion. There are many others that could be described. It will be recalled from chapter 5, for example, that researchers also have addressed how attribution and related concepts apply to the problems of institutionalized elderly persons (e.g., Langer & Rodin, 1976). It seems likely that this extension of basic abstractions to understand practical problems will continue, especially in light of the rapid movement of psychologists into the arena of health sciences. We view this extension as potentially quite fruitful. However, we hasten to caution that applications will have merit only to the extent that the linkages to basic process concepts are well-reasoned and articulated and that research designs meet reasonably high standards of scholarship (see Dingus, 1980, for a discussion of methodological problems involved in applying attribution ideas to psychotherapy).

Contemporary Issues

In this final section, we will identify a few central issues that confront attribution researchers in the 1980s.

Accuracy and Error

One quite salient issue concerns the accuracy of attributions. Attribution researchers perforce at some point in their analysis must be concerned with the veridicality of the explanations people offer for their own and others' behavior. An influential paper by Ross (1977) relates to this concern. Ross conceptualized and assimilated evidence about what he refers to as "the fundamental attribution error" which he defines as ". . . the tendency for attributors to underestimate the impact of situational factors and to overestimate the role of dispositional factors in controlling behavior" (p. 183). As Ross notes, Heider (1958) originally discusses this tendency as a cognitive error or bias, though importantly, he did not call it a *fundamental* error. Rather, Heider (1958) qualifies his position by suggesting that " . . . *under certain conditions,* there is a tendency to attribute the outcome of an action to the person, even though its source may reside in the environment" (p. 96, emphasis added). As theoretical and empirical work has evolved since the publication of Ross' paper, the fundamental attribution error has been uncritically treated as a central concept in the field by many investigators (e.g., Jones, Riggs, & Quattrone, 1979; Miller, Baer, & Schonberg, 1979).

It now even has been accorded the stature of topical heading in major textbooks in social psychology (Worchel & Cooper, 1979, p. 180) and person perception (Schneider, Hastorf, & Ellsworth, 1979). The term, therefore, seems to have become more than a hyperbole, whether or not it was meant as such.

As Kelley and Michela (1980) noted, however, this analysis and the accompanying research concerning the fundamental attribution error is susceptible to serious challenge regarding the development of defensible criteria of accuracy, "Of course, since the entire enterprise of psychology is directed toward specification of the true causes of behavior, and since the causes and their relative magnitudes are not yet known, it may be impossible to design a study to test unequivocally the accuracy of attribution" (p. 479).

In another critique of Ross' fundamental attribution error analysis, Harvey, Town, and Yarkin (in press) argued that the assumption that the pronounced tendency to make dispositional attributions represents a fundamental error in attribution is logically indefensible. They suggested that dispositional qualities may in fact represent reasonable explanations for behavior in some circumstances, and the general tendency to underestimate the importance of situational factors may be offset by certain demonstrable factors. Also, Harvey et al. contended there undoubtedly are situations in which it is just as plausible to argue that situational attributional tendencies represent errors as there are situations in which it can be argued that dispositional attributional tendencies represent errors. They concluded by questioning not only how the tendency Ross described can be considered "fundamental," but also what was meant by the concept of "error."

When and How People Naturally Make Attributions

The difficult matter of the various forms the attribution act takes, whether simple or complex, conscious or unconscious, automatic or deliberate, is, as Kelley and Michela (1980) suggested, one of the most imposing issues confronting attribution workers. Indeed, measurement of attributional activities represents a major problem in the field. It requires, in part, a theory about the nature of attributions, as well as when and how they occur naturally. Heider (1976) has suggested that people may spontaneously engage in considerable interpretation as they observe interpersonal events. However, analysts of attribution research using traditional techniques (e.g., Manis, 1977) have questioned the extent to which people are spontaneously interested in the causes that underlie behavior.

Although the type of theoretical advance noted above is not on the immediate horizon, there has been some work designed to probe relatively naturalistic attributional activity via unique methodologies. Typically, attribution researchers ask respondents to answer a series of questions about the extent to which such factors as self, situational forces, ability, and effort led to an outcome. However, Harvey, Yarkin, Lightner, and Town (1980) have pointed out that the request that a person make an attribution may influence the interpretive act in a way that would not ordinarily be characteristic of a naturalistic interpretation of the event observed. Harvey et al. presented evidence presumably showing relatively naturalistic attributional tendencies using what they called an "unsolicited attribution" paradigm. In this paradigm, respondents provided written accounts of what they saw and heard in observing the stimulus event; in some of the work, single thoughts were placed one per box. These written reports were coded by independent raters (and in one study by respondents too) for number and type of attributions made. Attributional evidence was reliably coded by both independent judges and respondents. The data deriving from the Harvey et al. research showed that individuals exhibited systematic patterns and magnitudes of attributional activity in this procedure which did not involve an explicit inquiry about causal inferences.

Other research that has investigated the efficacy of free response formats has been reported by Elig and Frieze (1974, 1979) and Wong and Weiner (1979). In general, the results of this work revealed that people exhibited discernible patterns of attributions about the causes of success and failure in hypothetical situations described to respondents. However, Elig and Frieze (1979) found that compared to structured scale measures, open-ended response measures had poor reliability. Indeed, despite the promise presented by the response formats in these studies, questions of replicability and intercoder reliability remain to be answered by future research.

Finally, Kelley and Michela (1980) offered a valuable comment regarding this issue of when and how people make attributions naturally. They noted that the frequent measurement problems derive in part from overly simplistic theoretical distinctions. But they observed that, as important, the problems also stemmed from inadequate study of the causal distinctions made by ordinary people.

A Final Note

As noted in chapter 1, attribution theory and research has had an immense impact on social psychology within the last decade, and it seems likely that attributional phenomena will continue to be a major focus of theoretical and empirical work. In this chapter, it has been suggested that we are likely to see an increase in attempts to integrate hitherto disparate systems and points of view. Further, we have suggested that in the future, we will see an increase in applications of attributional analyses to complex and important social settings and problems and an accompanying increase in theoretical and methodological sophistication. With greater emphasis upon complex phenomena and intricate methods for studying these phenomena, it may be difficult but important to remember that Heider's concern was with "a common-sense psychology," that is, a concern with phenomena that have meaning for and are phenomenologically real to individuals. As we become interested in the integrations of various systems within the perceiver and with more molar social processes which affect the individual, we will continue to focus on the psychological assumptions ordinary people use in giving meaning to their social environments. It may be, however, that the most tenable characterization of the contemporary human being will be that of a sophisticated attributor (at times rational or relatively unbiased, at times irrational or relatively biased) trying to cope with an intricate world of social relationships and events.

There is occasions and causes why and wherefore in all things. Shakespeare, *King Henry* V, v, i,[3]

References

Abelson, R. P. A script theory of understanding, attitude, and behavior. In J. S. Carroll & J. W. Payne (eds.), *Cognition and social behavior.* Hillsdale, N.J.: Erlbaum Associates, 1976.

Abramson, L. Y., Seligman, M. E. P., & Teasdale, J. D. Learned helplessness in humans: Critique and reformulation. *Journal of Abnormal Psychology,* 1978, *87*, 49-74.

Alloy, L. B. & Abramson, L. Y. Judgment of contingency in depressed and nondepressed students: Sadder but wiser? *Journal of Experimental Psychology: General,* 1979, *108*, 441-485.

The American Heritage Dictionary of the English Language. N.Y.: American Heritage Publishing Company, 1969.

Andreoli, V. A., Worchel, S., & Folger, R. Implied threat to behavioral freedom. *Journal of Personality and Social Psychology,* 1974, *30*, 765-771.

Armsby, R. E. A reexamination of the development of moral judgments in children. *Child Development,* 1971, *42*, 1241-1248.

Arnkoff, D. B., & Mahoney, M. J. The role of perceived control in psychotherapy. In L. C. Perlmuter & R. A. Monty (Eds.), *Choice and perceived control.* Hillsdale: Erlbaum, 1979.

Baldwin, C. P., & Baldwin, A. L. Children's judgments of kindness. *Child Development,* 1970, *41*, 29-47.

Bandura, A. *Principles of behavior modification.* New York: Holt, 1969.

Bandura, A. Self-efficacy: Toward a unifying theory of behavioral change. *Psychological Bulletin,* 1977, *84*, 191-215.

Bandura, A., Jeffrey, R. W., & Gajdos, E. Generalized change through participant modeling with self-directed mastery. *Behavior Research and Therapy,* 1975, *13*, 141-152.

Beck, A. T. *Depression: Clinical, experimental, and theoretical aspects.* New York: Harper & Row, 1967.

Bem, D. J. Reply to Judson Mills. *Psychological Review,* 1967, *74*, 536-537.

Bem, D. J. Self-perception: An alternative interpretation of cognitive dissonance phenomena. *Psychological Review,* 1967, *74*, 183-200.

Bem, D. J. Self-perception theory. In L. Berkowitz (ed.), *Advances in experimental social psychology* (Vol. 6). New York: Academic Press, 1972.

Bem, D. J., & McConnell, H. K. On the salience of premanipulation attitudes. *Journal of Personality and Social Psychology,* 1970, *14*, 23-31.

Benson, J. S., & Kennelly, K. J. Learned helplessness: The result of uncontrollable reinforcements or uncontrollable aversive stimulus? *Journal of Personality and Social Psychology,* 1976, *34*, 138-145.

Berg-Cross, L. G. Intentionality, degree of damage, and moral judgments. *Child Development,* 1975, *46*, 970-974.

Brendt, T. J., & Brendt, E. G. Children's use of motives and intentionality in person perception and moral judgment. *Child Development*, 1975, *46*, 904-912.

Bootzin, R. R., Herman, C. P., & Nicassio, P. The power of suggestion: Another examination of misattribution and insomnia. *Journal of Personality and Social Psychology*, 1976, *34*, 673-679.

Borgida, E. Scientific deduction—Evidence is not necessarily information: A reply to Wells and Harvey. *Journal of Personality and Social Psychology*, 1978, *36*, 477-482.

Bowers, K. S. Presenter in debate with Richard E. Nisbett "Introspective access to higher order cognitive processes: Do we tell more than we know?" Presented at the Meeting of the American Psychological Association, New York, 1979.

Brehm, J. W. *A theory of psychological reactance.* New York: Academic Press, 1966.

Brehm, J. W. *Responses to loss of freedom: A theory of psychological reactance.* Morristown, N.J.: General Learning Press, 1972.

Brehm, J. W., & Cohen, A. R. Re-evaluation of choice alternatives as a function of their number of qualitative similarity. Journal of *Abnormal and Social Psychology*, 1959, *58*, 373-378.

Brehm, J. W., & Cohen, A. *Explorations in cognitive dissonance.* New York: Wiley, 1962.

Brehm, S. S. *The application of social psychology to clinical practice.* Washington: Hemisphere, 1976.

Bromley, D. B. Natural language and the development of the self. In C. B. Keasey (Ed.), *Nebraska Symposium on Motivation, 1977* (Vol. 25). Lincoln: University of Nebraska Press, 1978.

Burns, D. B., & Beck, A. T. Cognitive behavior modification of mood disorders. In J. P. Foreyt & D. P. Rothjen (Eds.), *Cognitive behavior therapy.* New York: Plenum Press, 1978.

Buss, A. R. Causes and reasons in attribution theory: A conceptual critique. *Journal of Personality and Social Psychology*, 1978, *36*, 1311-1321.

Buss, A. R. On the relationship between causes and reasons. *Journal of Personality and Social Psychology*, 1979, *37*, 1458-1461.

Calder, B. J. Endogenous-exogenous versus internal-external attributions: Implications for the development of attribution theory. *Personality and Social Psychology Bulletin*, 1977, *3*, 400-406.

Calder, B. J., Ross, M., & Insko, C. A. Attitude change and attitude attribution: Effects of incentive, choice, and consequences. *Journal of Personality and Social Psychology*, 1973, *25*, 84-99.

Calveric, B. R. A developmental approach to conceptualizing others. Papers presented at the meeting of the American Psychological Association, New York City, September, 1979.

Calvert-Boyanowsky, J., & Leventhal, H. The role of information in attenuating behavioral responses to stress: A reinterpretation of the misattribution phenomenon. *Journal of Personality and Social Psychology*, 1975, *32*, 214-221.

Cantor, J. R., Zillmann, D., & Bryant, J. Enhancement of experienced sexual arousal in response to erotic stimuli through misattribution of unrelated residual excitation. *Journal of Personaility and Social Psychology*, 1975, *32*, 69-75.

Chandler, M. J., Greenspan, M., & Barenboim, C. Judgments of intentionality in response to videotaped and verbally presented moral dilemmas: The medium is the message. *Child Development*, 1973, *44*, 315-320.

Cohen, E. A. Gelfand, D. M., & Hartmann, D. P. Developmental differences in chil- ✓
dren's causal attributions. Paper presented at the meeting of the American Psychological Association, New York City, September, 1979.

Colletti, G., & Kopel, S. A. Maintaining behavior change: An investigation of three
maintenance strategies and the relationship of self-attribution to the long-
term reduction of cigarette smoking. *Journal of Consulting and Clinical
Psychology*, 1979, *47*, 614-617.

Collins, B. E., & Hoyt, M. F. Personal repsonsibility for consequences: An interaction
and extension of the "forced compliance" literature. *Journal of Experimental Social Psychology*, 1972, *8*, 558-593.

Conger, J. C., Conger, A. J., & Brehm, S. . Fear level as a moderator of false feedback
effects in snake phobics. *Journal of Consulting and Clinical Psychology*,
1976, *44*, 135-141.

Copple, C. E., & Coon, R. C. The role of causality in encoding and remembering
events as a function of age. *Journal of Genetic Psychology*, 1977, *130*,
129-136.

Costanzo, P. R., Coie, J. D., Grumet, J. E., & Farnhill, D. A re-examination of the
effects of intent and consequences on children's moral judgments. *Child
Development*, 1973, *44*, 154-161.

Costello, C. G. A critical review of Seligman's laboratory experiments on learned
helplessness and depression in humans. *Journal of Abnormal Psychology*, 1978, *87*, 21-31.

Cunningham, J. D., & Kelley, H. H. Causal attributions for interpersonal events of
varying magnitudes. *Journal of Personality*, 1975, *43*, 74-93.

Darley, J. M., & Latané, B. Bystander intervention in emergencies: Diffusion of responsibility. *Journal of Personality and Social Psychology*, 1968, *8*,
377-383.

Davison, A., & Steiner, I. D. Reinforcement schedules and attributed freedom. *Journal
of Personality and Social Psychology*, 1971, *19*, 357-366.

Davison, G. C., Tsujimoto, R. N., & Glaros, A. G. Attribution and the maintenance of
behavior change in falling asleep. *Journal of Abnormal Psychology*, 1973,
82, 124-133.

Davison, G., & Valins, S. Maintenance of self-attributed and drug-attributed behavior
change. *Journal of Personality and Social Psychology*, 1969, *11*, 25-33.

De Charms, R. *Personal causation.* New York: Academic Press, 1968.

Depue, R. A., & Monroe, S. M. Learned helplessness in the perspective of the depressive disorders: Conceptual and definitional issues. *Journal of Abnormal Psychology*, 1978, *87*, 3-20.

Dingus, C. M. Attribution therapy: A critique of the Schachterian model. Unpublished
manuscript, 1980.

Dweck, C. S. The role of expectations and attributions in the alleviation of learned
helplessness. *Journal of Personality and Social Psychology*, 1975, *31*,
674-685.

Dweck, C. S., & Goetz, T. E. Attributions and learned helplessness. In J. H. Harvey,
W. J. Ickes, & R. F. Kidd (Eds.), *New directions in attribution research*
(Vol. 2). Hillsdale: Erlbaum, 1978.

Dweck, C. S., & Repucci, N. D. Learned helplessness and reinforcement responsibility in children. *Journal of Personality and Social Psychology*, 1973, *25*,
109-116.

Dyck, R. J., & Rule, B. G. The effect on retaliation of causal attributions concerning
attack. *Journal of Personality and Social Psychology*, 1978, *36*, 521-529.

Elig, T. W., & Frieze, I. H. A multi-dimensional coding scheme of causal attributions
in social and academic situations. *Personality and Social Psychology
Bulletin*, 1974, *1*, 94-96.

⅄ Elig, T. W., & Frieze, I. H. Measuring causal attributions for success and failure. *Journal of Personality and Social Psychology,* 1979, *37,* 621–634.

Ellis, A. *Reason and emotion in psychotherapy.* New York: Lyle Stuart Press, 1962.

Farnill, D. The effects of social-judgment set on children's use of intent information. *Journal of Personality,* 1974, *42,* 276–289.

Festinger, L. *A theory of cognitive dissonance.* New York: Harper & Row, Publishers, 1957.

Fincham, F., & Jaspars, J. Attribution of responsibility to the self and other in children and adults. *Journal of Personality and Social Psychology,* 1979, *37,* 1589–1602.

Fischhoff, B. Attribution theory and judgment under uncertainty. In J. H. Harvey, W. J. Ickes, & R. F. Kidd (Eds.), *New directions in attribution research* (Vol. 1). Hillsdale, N.J.: Erlbaum Associates, 1976.

Frieze, I. H., Bar-Tal, D., & Carroll, J. S. (Eds.). *New approaches to social problems: Applications of attribution theory.* San Francisco: Jossey-Bass Inc., 1979.

✓ Frieze, I., & Weiner, B. Cue utilization and attributional judgments for success and failure. *Journal of Personality,* 1971, *39,* 591–606.

Fromm, E. *Escape from freedom.* New York: Holt, Rinehart and Winston, Inc., 1941.

Gaupp, L. A., Stern, R. M., & Galbraith, G. G. False heart-rate feedback and reciprocal inhibition by aversive relief in the treatment of snake avoidance behavior. *Behavior Therapy,* 1972, *3,* 7–20.

Glass, D. C., & Singer, J. E. *Urban stress: Experiments on noise and social stressors.* New York: Academic Press, 1972.

Glass, D. C., Singer, J. E., & Friedman, L. N. Psychic cost of adaptation to an environmental stressor. *Journal of Personality and Social Psychology,* 1969, *12,* 200–210.

Gould, R., & Sigall, H. The effects of empathy and outcome on attribution: An examination of the divergent perspectives hypothesis. *Journal of Experimental Social Psychology,* 1977, *13,* 480–491.

Greene, D., & Lepper, M. R. Effects of extrinsic rewards on children's subsequent intrinsic interest. *Child Development,* 1974, *45,* 1141–1145.

Guttentag, M., & Longfellow, C. Children's social attributions: Development and change. In C. B. Keasey (Ed.), *Nebraska Symposium on Motivation, 1977* (Vol. 25). Lincoln: University of Nebraska Press, 1978.

Hansen, R. D., & Donoghue, J. M. The power of consensus: Information derived from one's own and other's behavior. *Journal of Personality and Social Psychology,* 1977, *35,* 294–302.

Harré, R. Expressive aspects of descriptions of others. In C. Antaki (Ed.), *The psychology of ordinary explanations of social behaviour.* London: Academic Press, in press.

Harris, B. Developmental differences in the attribution of responsibility. *Developmental Psychology,* 1977, *13,* 257–265.

Harris, B., & Harvey, J. H. Attribution theory: From phenomenal causality to the intuitive social scientist and beyond. In C. Antaki (Ed.), *The psychology of ordinary explanations of social behaviour.* London: Academic Press, in press.

Harris, B., & Harvey, J. H. Self-attributed choice as a function of the consequence of a decision. *Journal of Personality and Social Psychology,* 1975, *31,* 1013–1019.

Harvey, J. H., Arkin, R. M., Gleason, J. M., & Johnston, S. Effect of expected and observed outcome of an action on the differential causal attributions of actor and observer. *Journal of Personality,* 1974, *42,* 62–77.

Harvey, J. H., Barnes, R. D., Sperry, D. L., & Harris, B. Perceived choice as a function of internal-external locus of control. *Journal of Personality,* 1974, *42,* 437-452.

Harvey, J. H., & Harris, B. Determinants of perceived choice and the relationship between perceived choice and the expectancy about feelings of internal control. *Journal of Personality and Social Psychology,* 1975, *31,* 101-106.

Harvey, J. H., Harris, B., & Barnes, R. D. Actor-observer differences in the perceptions of responsibility and freedom. *Journal of Personality and Social Psychology,* 1975, *32,* 22-28.

Harvey, J. H., Harris, B., & Lightner, J. M. Perceived freedom as a central concept in psychological theory and research. In L. C. Perlmuter & R. A. Monty (Eds.), *Choice and perceived control.* Hillsdale, N.J.: Lawrence Erlbaum Associates, 1979.

Harvey, J. H., & Jellison, J. M. Determinants of perceived choice, number of options, and perceived time in making a selection. *Memory & Cognition,* 1974, *2,* 539-544.

Harvey, J. H., & Johnston, S. Determinants of the perception of choice. *Journal of Experimental Social Psychology,* 1973, *9,* 164-179.

Harvey, J. H., & Smith, W. P. *Social psychology: An attributional approach.* St. Louis: C. V. Mosby, 1977.

Harvey, J. H., Town, J. P., & Yarkin, K. L. How fundamental is "The fundamental attribution error?" *Journal of Personality and Social Psychology: Personality Processes and Individual Differences,* in press.

Harvey, J. H., & Tucker, J. A. On problems with the cause-reason distinction in attribution theory. *Journal of Personality and Social Psychology,* 1979, *37,* 1441-1446.

Harvey, J. H., Wells, G. L., & Alvarez, M. D. Attribution in the context of conflict and separation in close relationships. In J. H. Harvey, W. Ickes, & R. F. Kidd (Eds.), *New directions in attribution research* (Vol. 2). Hillsdale, N.J.: Lawrence Erlbaum Associates, 1978.

Harvey, J. H., Yarkin, K. L., Lightner, J. M., & Town, J P. Unsolicited interpretation and recall of interpersonal events. *Journal of Personality and Social Psychology: Attitudes and Social Cognition,* 1980, *38,* 551-568.

Hastie, R., Ostrom, T. M., Ebbesen, E. B., Wyer, R. S., Hamilton, D. L., & Carlston, D. E. *Person memory: Cognitive basis of social perception.* Hillsdale, N.J.: Lawrence Erlbaum Associates, 1980.

Heider, F. Social perception and phenomenal causality. *Psychological Review,* 1944, *51,* 358-374.

Heider, F. *The psychology of interpersonal relations.* New York: John Wiley & Sons, 1958.

Heider, F. A conversation with Fritz Heider. In J. H. Harvey, W. J. Ickes, & R. F. Kidd (Eds.), *New directions in attribution research* (Vol. 1). Hillsdale, N.J.: Erlbaum Associates, 1976.

Heider, F. The function of the perceptual system. *Psychological Issues,* 1959, *1,* 35-52.

Hiroto, D. S. Locus of control and learned helplessness. *Jorunal of Experimental Psychology,* 1974, *102,* 187-193.

Hiroto, D. S., & Seligman, M. E. P. Generality of learned helplessness in man. *Journal of Personality and Social Psychology,* 1975, *31,* 311-327.

Hoffman, M. L. Moral development. In P. H. Mussen (Ed.), *Carmichael's manual of child psychology* (3rd ed.; Vol. 2). New York: Wiley, 1970.

Ickes, W. J., & Kidd, R. F. Attributional analysis of helping behavior. In J. H. Harvey, W. J. Ickes, & R. F. Kidd (Eds.), *New directions in attribution research* (Vol. 1). Hillsdale, N.J.: Lawrence Erlbaum Associates, 1976.

Imamoglu, E. O. Children's awareness and usage of intention cues. *Child Development,* 1975, *46,* 39-45.

Jellison, J. M., & Harvey, J. H. Determinants of perceived choice and the relationship between perceived choice and perceived competence. *Journal of Personality and Social Psychology,* 1973, *28,* 376-382.

Jones, E. E. A conversation with Edward E. Jones and Harold H. Kelley. In J. H. Harvey, W. Ickes, & R. F. Kidd (Eds.), *New directions in attribution research* (Vol. 2). Hillsdale, N.J.: Lawrence Erlbaum Associates, 1978.

Jones, E. E., & Davis, K. E. From acts to dispositions: The attribution process in person perception. In L. Berkowitz (Ed.), *Advances in experimental social psychology* (Vol. 2). New York: Academic Press, 1965.

Jones, E. E., Davis, K. E., & Gergen, K. J. Role playing variations and their informational value for person perception. *Journal of Abnormal and Social Psychology,* 1961, *63,* 302-310.

Jones, E. E., & Harris, V. A. The attribution of attitudes. *Journal of Experimental Social Psychology,* 1967, *3,* 1-24.

Jones, E. E., & Kelley, H. H. A conversation with Edward E. Jones and Harold H. Kelley. In J. H. Harvey, W. Ickes, & R. F. Kidd (Eds.), *New directions in attribution research* (Vol. 2). Hillsdale, N.J.: Lawrence Erlbaum Associates, 1978.

Jones, E. E., & McGillis, D. Correspondent inferences and the attribution cube: A comparative reappraisal. In J. H. Harvey, W. J. Ickes, & R. F. Kidd (Eds.), *New directions in attribution research* (Vol. 1). Hillsdale, N.J.: Erlbaum Associates, 1976, 389-420.

Jones, E. E., & Nisbett, R. E. The actor and the observer: Divergent perceptions of the causes of behavior. In E. E. Jones, D. E. Kanouse, H. H. Kelley, R. E. Nisbett, S. Valins, & B. Weiner (Eds.), *Attribution: Perceiving the causes of behavior.* Morristown, N.J.: General Learning Press, 1972.

Jones, E. E., Riggs, J. M., & Quattrone, G. Observer bias in the attitude attribution paradigm: Effect of time and information order. *Journal of Personality and Social Psychology,* 1979, *37,* 1230-1238.

Jones, E. E., & Thibaut, J. W. Interaction goals as bases of inference in person perception. In R. Tagiuri & L. Petrullo (Eds.), *Person perception and interpersonal behavior.* Standford, Calif.: Standford University Press, 1955.

Jones, E. E., Worchel, S., Goethals, G. R., & Grumet, J. F. Prior expectancy and behavioral extremity as determinants of attitude attribution. *Journal of Experimental Social Psychology,* 1971, *7,* 59-80.

Jones, R. A., Linder, D. E., Kiesler, C. A., Zanna, M., & Brehm, J. W. Internal states or external stimuli: Observers' attitude judgments and the dissonance theory-self-persuasion controversy. *Journal of Experimental Social Psychology,* 1968, *4,* 247-269.

Karniol, R. Children's use of intention cues in evaluating behavior. *Psychological Bulletin,* 1978, *85,* 76-85.

Karniol, R., & Ross, M. Children's use of causal attribution schema and the inference of manipulative intentions. *Child Development,* 1979, *50,* 463-468.

Karniol, R., & Ross, M. The development of causal attributions in social perception. *Journal of Personality and Social Psychology,* 1976, *34,* 455-464.

Kassin, S. M. Consensus information, prediction, and causal attribution: A review of the literature and issues. *Journal of Personality and Social Psychology,* 1979, *37,* 1966-1981.

Keasey, C. B. Young children's attribution of intentionality to themselves and others. *Child Development,* 1977, *48,* 261-264.

Keasey, C. B. Children's developing awareness and usage of intentionality and motives. In C. B. Keasey (Ed.), *Nebraska Symposium on Motivation, 1977* (Vol. 25). Lincoln: University of Nebraska Press, 1978.

Kehoe, J. F. Choice time and aspects of choice alternatives. In L. C. Perlmuter and R. A. Monty (Eds.), *Choice and perceived control.* Hillsdale, N.J.: Lawrence Erlbaum Assoicates, 1979.

Kelley, H. H. Attribution theory in social psychology. In D. Levine (Ed.), *Nebraska symposium on motivation* (Vol. 15). Lincoln: University of Nebraska Press, 1967.

Kelley, H. H. Causal schemata and the attribution process. In E. E. Jones, D. E. Kanouse, H. H. Kelley, R. E. Nisbett, S. Valins, and B. Weiner (Eds.), *Attribution: Perceiving the causes of behavior.* Morristown, N.J.: General Learning Press, 1972(a).

Kelley, H. H. Attribution in social interaction. In E. E. Jones, D. E. Kanouse, H. H. Kelley, R. E. Nisbett, S. Valins, & B. Weiner (Eds.), *Attribution: Perceiving the causes of behavior.* Morristown, N.J.: General Learning Press, 1972(b).

Kelley, H. H. A conversation with Edward E. Jones and Harold H. Kelley. In J. H. Harvey, W. Ickes, & R. F. Kidd (Eds.), *New directions in attribution research* (Vol. 2). Hillsdale, N.J.: Erlbaum Associates, 1978, 371-387.

Kelley, H. H., & Michela, J. L. Attribution theory and research. *Annual Review of Psychology,* 1980, 31, 457-501.

Kellogg, R., & Baron, R. S. Attribution theory, insomnia, and the reverse placebo effect: A reversal of Storms and Nisbett's findings. *Journal of Personality and Social Psychology,* 1975, *32,* 231-236.

Kent, R. N., Wilson, G. T., & Nelson, R. Effects of false heart-rate feedback on avoidance behavior: An investigation of "cognitive desensitization." *Behavior Therapy,* 1972, *3,* 1-6.

King, M. The development of some intention concepts in young children. *Child Development,* 1971, *42,* 1145-1152.

Klein, D. C., Fencil-Morse, E., & Seligman, M.E. P. Learned helplessness, depression, and the attribution of failure. *Journal of Personality and Social Psychology,* 1976, *33,* 508-516.

Koeske, G. F., & Koeske, R. K. Deviance and a generalized disposition toward internality: An attributional approach. *Journal of Personality,* 1975, *43,* 634-646.

Kopel, S., & Arkowitz, H. The role of attribution and self-perception in behavior change: Implications for behavior therapy. *Genetic Psychology Monographs,* 1975, *92,* 175-212.

Kruglanski, A. W. The endogenous-exogenous partition in attribution theory. *Psychological Review,* 1975, *82,* 387-406.

Kruglanski, A. W. The place of naive contents in a theory of attribution: Reflections on Calder's and Zuckerman's critiques of the endogenous-exogenous partition. *Personality and Social Psychology Bulletin,* 1977, *3,* 592-605.

Kruglanski, A. W. Causal explanation, teleological explanation: On radical particularism in attribution theory. *Journal of Personality and Social Psychology,* 1979, 1447-1457.

Kruglanski, A. W., & Cohen, M. Attributed freedom and personal causation. *Journal of Personality and Social Psychology,* 1973, *26,* 245-250.

Kruglanski, A. W., Hamel, I. Z., Maides, S. A., & Schwartz, J. M. Attribution theory as a special case of lay epistemology. In J. H. Harvey, W. J. Ickes, & R. F. Kidd (Eds.), *New directions in attribution research (Vol. 2). Hillsdale, N.J.: Erlbaum Associates, 1978, 299-333.*

Kuiper, N. A. Depression and causal attributions for success and failure. *Journal of Personality and Social Psychology,* 1978, *36,* 236-246.

Langer, E. J. The illusion of control. *Journal of Personality and Social Psychology,* 1975, *32,* 311-328.

Langer, E. J. The illusion of incompetence. In L. C. Perlmuter, & R. A. Monty (Eds.), *Choice and perceived control.* Hillsdale, N.J.: Lawrence Erlbaum Associates, 1979.

Langer, E. J. Rethinking the role of thought in social interaction. In J. H. Harvey, W. J. Ickes, & R. F. Kidd (Eds.), *New directions in attribution research* (Vol. 2). Hillsdale, N.J.: Erlbaum Associates, 1978.

Langer, E. J., & Benevento, A. Self-induced dependence. *Journal of Personality and Social Psychology,* 1978, *36,* 886-893.

Langer, E., Blank, A., & Chanowitz, B. The mindlessness of ostensibly thoughtful action: The role of "placebic" information in interpersonal interaction. *Journal of Personality and Social Psychology,* 1978, *36,* 635-642.

Langer, E., & Newman, H. M. The role of mindlessness in a typical social psychological experiment. *Personality and Social Psychology Bulletin,* 1979, *5,* 295-298.

Langer, E. J., & Rodin, J. The effects of choice and enhanced personal responsibility for the aged: A field experiment in an institutional setting. *Journal of Personality and Social Psychology* 1976, *34,* 191-198.

Lepper M. R., Greene, D., & Nisbett, R. E. Undermining children's intrinsic interest with extrinsic rewards: A test of the "overjustification" hypothesis. *Journal of Personality and Social Psychology,* 1973, *28,* 129-137.

Leventhal, H. Emotions: A basic problem for social psychology. In C. Nemeth (Ed.), *Social Psychology: Classic and contemporary integrations.* Chicago: Rnad McNally, 1974.

Leventhal, H., Brown, D., Shacham, S., & Engquist, G. Effects of preparatory information about sensations. Threat of pain, and attention on cold pressor distress. *Journal of Personality and Social Psychology,* 1979, *37,* 688-714.

Livesley, W. J., & Bromley, D. B. *Person perception in childhood and adolescence.* London: Wiley, 1973.

London, H., & Nisbett, R. E. (Eds.), *Cognitive alterations of feeling states.* Chicago: Aldine, 1974.

Maier, S. F., & Seligman, M. E. P. Learned helplessness: Theory and evidence. *Journal of Experimental Psychology,* 1976, *105,* 3-46.

Manis, M. Cognitive social psychology. *Personality and Social Psychology Bulletin,* 1977, *3,* 550-566.

Marshall, G. D., & Zimbardo, P. G. Affective consequences of inadequately explained physiological arousal. *Journal of Personality and Social Psychology,* 1979, *37,* 970-988.

Maslach, C. Negative emotional biasing of unexplained arousal. *Journal of Personality and Social Psychology,* 1979, *37,* 953-969.

McArthur, L. A. The how and what of why: Some determinants and consequences of causal attribution. *Journal of Personality and Social Psychology,* 1972, *22,* 171-193.

Mead, G. H. *Mind, self, and society.* Chicago: University of Chicago Press, 1934.

Meichenbaum, D. *Cognitive-behavior modification: An integrative approach.* New York: Plenum, 1977.

Miller, A. G., Baer, R., & Schonberg, P. The bias phenomenon in attribution: Actor and observer perspectives. *Journal of Personality and Social Psychology,* 1979, *37,* 1421-1431.

Miller, D. T. What constitutes a self-serving attributional bias?: A reply to Bradley. *Journal of Personality and Social Psychology*, 1978, *36*, 1221-1223.

Miller, D. T., & Ross, M. Self-serving bases in the attribution of causality: Fact or fiction? *Psychological Bulletin,* 1975, *82*, 213-215.

Miller, I. W., & Norman, W. H. Learned helplessness in humans: A review and attribution-theory model. *Psychological Bulletin,* 1979, *86*, 93-118.

Miller, R., Brickman, P., & Bolen, D. Attribution versus persuasion as a means for modifying behavior. *Journal of Personality and Social Psychology*, 1975, *31*, 430-441.

Mills, J. Comment on Bem's "self-perception: An alternative interpretation of cognitive dissonance phenomena." *Psychological Review*, 1967, *74*, 535.

Mills, J. *Unpublished analysis of perceived choice.* University of Missouri-Columbia, 1970.

Monson, T. C., & Snyder, M. Actors, observers, and the attribution process: Toward a reconceptualization. *Journal of Experimental Social Psychology*, 1977, *13*, 89-111.

Newtson, D. Dispositional inference from effects of actions: Effects chosen and effects foregone. *Journal of Experimental Social Psychology*, 1974, *10*, 489-496.

Nisbett, R. E., & Borgida, E. Attribution and the psychology of prediction. *Journal of Personality and Social Psychology*, 1975, *32*, 932-943.

Nisbett, R. E., Borgida, E., Crandall, R., & Reed, H. Popular induction: Information is not always informative. In J. S. Carroll, & J. W. Payne (Eds.), *Cognitive and social behavior.* Hillsdale, N.J.: Erlbaum Associates, 1976.

Nisbett, R. E., Caputo, C., Legant, P., & Marecek, J. Behavior as seen by the actor and as seen by the observer. *Journal of Personality and Social Psychology*, 1973, *27*, 154-164.

Nisbett, R. E., & Schachter, S. Cognitive manipulation of pain. *Journal of Experimental Social Psychology*, 1966, *2*, 227-236.

Nisbett, R. E., & Wilson, T. D. Telling more than we can know: Verbal reports on mental processes. *Psychological Review*, 1977, *84*, 231-259.

Nummedal, S. G., & Bass, S. C. Effects of the salience of intention and consequence on children's moral judgments. *Developmental Psychology*, 1976, *12*, 475-476.

Orvis, B. R., Cunningham, J. D., & Kelley, H. H. A closer examination of causal inference: The roles of consensus, distinctiveness, and consistency information. *Journal of Personality and Social Psychology*, 1975, *32*, 605-616.

Orvis, B.R., Kelley, H. H., & Butler, D. Attributional conflict in young couples. In J. H. Harvey, W. J. Ickes, & R. F. Kidd (Eds.), *New directions in attribution research* (Vol. 1). Hillsdale, N.J.: Erlbaum Associates, 1976.

Ostrove, N. Expectations for success on effort-determined tasks as a function of incentive and performance feedback. *Journal of Personality and Social Psychology*, 1978, *36*, 909-916.

Overmier, J. B., & Seligman, M. E. P. Effects of inescapable shock upon subsequent escape and avoidance learning. *Journal of Comparative and Physiological Psychology*, 1967, *63*, 23-33.

The Oxford English Dictionary. Oxford: Oxford University Press, 1933.

Perlmuter, L. C., & Monty, R. A. (Eds.), *Choice and perceived control.* Hillsdale, N.J.: Lawrence Erlbaum Associates, 1979.

Perlmuter, L. C., Monty, R. A., & Kimble, G. A. Effect of choice on paired-associate learning. *Journal of Experimental Psychology*, 1971, *91*, 47-53.

Phares, E. J., & Wilson, K. G. Responsibility attribution: Role of outcome severity, situational ambiguity, and internal-external control. *Journal of Personality*, 1972, *40*, 392-406.

Piaget, J. *The moral judgment of the child*. New York: Harcourt, Brace, 1932.

Regan, D. T. Attributional aspects of interpersonal attraction. In J. H. Harvey, W. J. Ickes, & R. F. Kidd (Eds.), *New directions in attribution research* (Vol. 2). Hillsdale, N.J.: Lawrence Erlbaum Associates, 1978.

Regan, D. R., & Totten, J. Empathy and attribution: Turning observers into actors. *Journal of Personality and Social Psychology*, 1975, *32*, 850-856.

Rest, S., Nierenberg, R., Weiner, B., & Heckhausen, H. Further evidence concerning the effects of perceptions of effort and ability on achievement evaluation. *Journal of Personality and Social Psycholoy*, 1973, *28*, 187-191.

Rich, M. C. Verbal reports on mental processes: Issues of accuracy and awareness. *Journal for the Theory of Social Behavior*, 1979, *9*, 29-37.

Rizley, R. Depression and distortion in the attribution of causality. *Journal of Abnormal Psychology*, 1978, *87*, 32-48.

Rodin, J., & Langer, E. J. Long-term effects of a control-relevant intervention with the institutionalized aged. *Journal of Personality and Social Psychology*, 1977, *35*, 897-902.

Ross, L. The intuitive psychologist and his shortcomings: Distortions in the attribution process. In. L. Berkowitz (Ed.), *Advances in experimental social psychology* (vol. 9l. 12). New York: Academic Press, 1977.

Ross, L., Rodin, J., & Zimbardo, P. G. Toward an attribution therapy: The reduction of fear through induced cognitive-emotional misattribution. *Journal of Personality and Social Psychology*, 1969, *12*, 279-288.

Ross, M. Salience of reward and intrinsic motivation. *Journal of Personality and Social Psychology*, 1975, *32*, 245-254.

Roth, S., & Bootzin, R. R. Effects of experimentally induced expectancies of external control: An investigation of learned helplessness. *Journal of Personality and Social Psychology*, 1974, *29*, 253-264.

Roth, S., & Kubal, L. Effects of non-contingent reinforcement on tasks of differing importance: Facilitation and learned helplessness. *Journal of Personality and Social Psychology*, 1975, *32*, 680-691.

Rotter, J. B. Generalized expectancies for internal versus external control of reinforcement. *Psychological Monographs*, 1966, *80* (1 Whole No. 609).

Ruble, D. N., & Feldman, N. S. Order of consensus, distinctiveness, and consistency information and causal attributions. *Journal of Personality and Social Psychology*, 1976, *34*, 930-937.

Schachter, S. The interaction of cognitive and physiological determinants of emotional state. In L. Berkowitz (Ed.), *Advances in experimental social psychology*. New York: Academic Press, 1964.

Schachter, S., & Singer, J. E. Cognitive, social, and physiological determinants of emotional state. *Psychological Review*, 1962, *69*, 379-399.

Schachter, S., & Singer, J. E. Comments on the Maslach and Marshall-Zimbardo experiments. *Journal of Personality and Social Psychology*, 1979, *37*, 989-995.

Schneider, D., Hastorf, A., & Ellsworth, P. *Person perception* (2nd edition). Reading, Mass.: Addison-Wesley Publishing Co., 1979.

Schulz, R. The effects of control predictability on the physical and psychological well-being of the institutionalized aged. *Journal of Personality and Social Psychology*, 1976, *33*, 563-573.

Secord, P., & Peevers, B. The development and attribution of person concepts. In T. Mischel (Ed.), *Understanding other persons*. Oxford: Blackwell, Basil & Mott, 1974.

Seligman, M. E. P. Fall into helplessness. *Psychology Today*, June, 1973, 43-48.

Seligman, M. E. P. *Helplessness: On depression, development, and death*. San Francisco: Freeman, 1975.

Seligman, M. E. P., Abramson, L. Y., Semmel, A., & Von Baeyer, C. Depressive attributional style. *Journal of Abnormal Psychology,* 1979, *88,* 242-247.

Seligman, M. E. P., & Maier, S. F. Failure to escape traumatic shock. *Journal of Experimental Psychology,* 1967, *74,* 1-9.

Seligman, M. E. P., Maier, S. F., & Geer, J. The alleviation of learned helplessness in the dog. *Journal of Abnormal and Social Psychology,* 1968, *73,* 256-262.

Seligman, M. E. P., Maier, S. F., & Soloman, R. L. Unpredictable and uncontrollable aversive events. In F. R. Brush (Ed.), *Aversive conditioning and learning.* New York: Academic Press, 1971.

Seligman, M. E. P., & Miller, S. M. The psychology of power: Concluding comments. In L. C. Perlmuter & R. A. Monty (Eds.), *Choice and perceived control.* Hillsdale, N.J.: Lawrence Erlbaum Associates, 1979.

Sensenig, S., & Brehm, J. W. Attitude change from an implied threat to attitudinal freedom. *Journal of Personality and Social Psychology,* 1968, *8,* 324-330.

Shaver, K. G *An introduction to attribution processes.* Cambridge: Winthrop, 1975.

Shaver, K. G. The land is fertile, but the farmers need a cooperative. *Contemporary Psychologist,* 1979, *24,* 680-682.

Shaver, K. G. Back to basics: On the role of theory in the attribution of causality. In J. H. Harvey, W. Ickes, & R. F. Kidd (Eds.), *New directions in attribution research* (Vol. 3). Hillsdale, N.J.: Lawrence Erlbaum Associates, in press.

Shaw, M. E., Bristoe, M. E., & Garcia-Esteve, J. A cross-cultural study of attribution of responsibility. *International Journal of Psychology,* 1968, *3,* 51-60.

Shaw, M. E., & Iwawaki, S. Attribution of responsibility by Japanese and Americans as a function of age. *Journal of Cross-Cultural Psychology,* 1972, *3,* 71-81.

Shaw, M. E., & Schneider, R. W. Intellectual competence as a variable in attribution of responsibility and assignment of sanctions. *Journal of Social Psychology,* 1969, *78,* 31-39.

Shaw, M. E., & Sulzer, J. L. An empirical test of Heider's levels of attribution of responsibility. *Journal of Abnormal Social Psychology,* 1964, *69,* 39-46.

Shotter, J. Telling and reporting: Prospective and retrospective uses of self-ascriptions. In C. Antaki (Ed.), *The psychology of ordinary explanations of social behaviour.* London: Academic Press, in press.

Shultz, T. R., Butkowsky, I., Pearce, J. W., & Shanfield, H. Development of schemes for the attribution of multiple psychological causes. *Developmental Psychology,* 1975, *11,* 502-510.

Sigall, H., & Michela, J. I'll bet you say that to all the girls: Physical attractiveness and reactions to praise. *Journal of Personality,* 1976, *44,* 611-626.

Singerman, K. G., Borkovec, T. D., & Baron, R. S. Failure of a misattribution therapy manipulation with a clinically relevant target behavior. *Behavior Therapy,* 1976, *7,* 306-313.

Skinner, B. F. *Beyond freedom and dignity.* New York: Knopf, 1971.

Smith, C. L., Gelfand, D. M., Hartmann, D. P., & Partlow, M. E. Y. Children's causal attributions regarding help giving. *Child Development,* 1979, *50,* 203-210.

Smith, E. R., & Miller F. D. Limits on perception of cognitive processes: A reply to Nisbett and Wilson. *Psychological Review,* 1978, *85,* 355-362.

Smith, M. C. Children's use of the multiple sufficient scheme in social perception. *Journal of Personality and Social Psychology,* 1975, *32,* 737-747.

Snyder, M. Attribution and behavior: Social perception and social causation. In J. H. Harvey, W. J. Ickes, & R. F. Kidd (Eds.), *New directions in attribution research* (Vol 1). Hillsdale, N.J.: Lawrence Erlbaum Associates, 1976.

Snyder, M., & Gangestad, S. Hypothesis-testing processes. In J. H. Harvey, W. Ickes, & R. F. Kidd (Eds.), *New directions in attribution research* (Vol. 3). Hillsdale, N.J.: Lawrence Erlbaum Associates, in press.

Snyder, M., & Swann, W. Behavioral confirmation in social interaction: From social perception to social reality. *Journal of Experimental Social Psychology,* 1978, *14,* 148–162.

Snyder, M., Tanke, E. D., & Berscheid, E. Social perception and interpersonal behavior: On the self-fulfilling nature of social stereotypes. *Journal of Personality and Social Psychology,* 1977, *35,* 656–666.

Steiner, I. D. Perceived freedom. In L. Berkowitz (Ed.), *Advances in experimental social psychology* (Vol. 5). New York: Academic Press, 1970.

Steiner, I. D. Three kinds of reported choice. In L. C. Perlmuter & R. A. Monty (Eds.), *Choice and perceived control.* Hillsdale, N.J.: Lawrence Erlbaum Associates, 1979.

Steiner, I. D., & Field, W. L. Role assignment and interpersonal influence. *Journal of Abnormal and Social Psychology,* 1960, *61,* 239–246.

Stern, R. M., Botto, R. W., & Herrick, C. D. Behavioral and physiological effects of false heart rate feedback: A replication and extension. *Psychophysiology,* 1972, *9,* 21–29.

Storms, M. D. Videotape and the attribution process: Reversing actors' and observers' points of view. *Journal of Personality and Social Psychology,* 1973, *27,* 165–175.

Storms, M. D., & McCaul, K. D. Attribution proceses and emotional exacerbation of dysfunctional behavior. In J. H. Harvey, W. J. Ickes, & R. F. Kidd (Eds.), *New directions in attribution research* (Vol. 1). Hillsdale: Erlbaum, 1976.

Storms, M. D., & McCaul, K. D. Stuttering, attribution, and exacerbation. Unpublished manuscript, University of Kansas, 1975.

Storms, M., & Nisbett, R. E. Insomnia and the attribution process. *Journal of Personality and Social Psychology,* 1970 *16,* 319–328.

Strong, S. R. Social psychological approaches to psychotherapy research. In A. E. Bergin, & S. L. Garfield (Eds.), *Handbook of psychotherapy research* (2nd edition). New York: Wiley, 1978.

Stryker, S. Developments in "two psychologies": Toward an appreciation of mutual relevance. *Sociometry,* 1977, *40,* 145–160.

Stryker, S., & Gottlieb, A. Attribution theory and symbolic interactionism: A comparison. In J. H. Harvey, W. Ickes, & R. F. Kidd (Eds.), *New directions in attribution research* (Vol. 3). Hillsdale, N.J.: Lawrence Erlbaum Associates, in press.

Sushinsky, L. S., & Bootzin, R. R. Cognitive desensitization as a model of systematic desensitization. *Behavior Research and Therapy,* 1970, *8,* 29–33.

Taylor, S. E., & Fiske, S. T. Salience, attention, and attribution: Top of the head phenomena. In L. Berkowitz (Ed.), *Advances in experimental social psychology* (Vol. 11). New York: Academic Press, 1978.

Thibaut, J. W., & Riecken, H. W. Some determinants and consequences of the perception of social causality. *Journal of Personality,* 1955, *24,* 113–133.

Thomas, W. I., & Thomas, D. S. *The child in America.* New York: Knopf, 1928.

Toffler, A. *Future shock.* New York: Bantam Books, 1970.

Valins, S. Cognitive effects of false heart-rate feedback. *Journal of Personality and Social Psychology,* 1966, *4,* 400–408.

Valins, S., & Nisbett, R. E. Attribution processes in the development and treatment of emotional disorders. In E. E. Jones, D. E. Kanouse, H. H. Kelley, (Eds.), *Attribution: Perceiving the causes of behavior.* Morristown, N.J.: General Learning Press, 1972.

Valins, S., & Ray, A. Effects of cognitive desensitization on avoidance behavior. *Journal of Personality and Social Psychology,* 1967, *20,* 239-250.

Weary Bradley, G. Self-serving biases in the attribution process: A reexamination of the fact or fiction question. *Journal of Personality and Social Psychology,* 1978, *36,* 56-71.

Weary, G. Self-serving attributional biases: Perceptive or response distortions? *Journal of Personality and Social Psychology,* 197, *37,* 1418-1420.

Weary, G. Affect and egotism as mediator of bias in causal attributions. *Journal of Personality and Social Psychology,* 1980, *38,* 348-357.

Weary, G., & Arkin, R. M Attributional self-presentation. In J. H. Harvey, W. Ickes, & R. F. Kidd (Eds.), *New directions in attribution research* (Vol. 3). Hillsdale, N.J.: Lawrence Erlbaum Associates, in press.

Webster's Seventh New Collegiate Dictionary. Springfield: G. & C. Merriam Company, 1963.

Weiner, B. From each according to his abilities: The role of effort in a moral society. *Human Development,* 1973, *16,* 53-60.

Weiner, B. *Achievement motivation and attribution theory.* Morristown, N.J.: General Learning Corp., 1974.

Weiner, B. A theory of motivation for some classroom experiences. *Journal of Educational Psychology,* 1979, *71,* 3-25.

Weiner, B., Frieze, I., Kukla, A., Reed, L., Rest, S., & Rosenbaum, R. M. Perceiving the causes of success and failure. In E. E. Jones, D. E. Kanouse, H. H. Kelley, R. E. Nisbett, S. Valins, & B. Weiner (Eds.), *Attribution: Perceiving the causes of behavior.* Morristown, N.J.: General Learning Press, 1972.

Weiner, B., Russell, D., & Lerman, D. Affective consequences of causal ascriptions. In J. H. Harvey, W. J. Ickes, & R. F. Kidd (Eds.), *New directions in attribution research* (Vol. 2). Hillsdale, N.J.: Erlbaum Associates, 1978, 59-90.

Weiss, R. S. *Marital separation.* New Yok: Basic Books, 1975.

Wells G. L., & Harvey, J. H. Do people use consensus information in making causal attributions? *Journal of Personality and Social Psychology,* 1977, *35,* 279-293.

Wells, G. L., & Harvey, J. H. Naive attributors' attributions and predictions: What is informative and when is an effect an effect? *Journal of Personality and Social Psychology,* 1978, *36,* 483-490.

Wells, G. L., Petty, R. E., Harkins, S. G., Kagehiro, D., & Harvey, J. H. Anticipated discussion of interpretation eliminates actor-observer differences in the attribution of causality. *Sociometry,* 1977, *46,* 247-253.

Whalen, C. K., & Henker, B. Psychostimulants and children: A review and analysis. *Psychological Bulletin,* 1976, *83,* 1113-1130.

White, P. Limitations on verbal reports of internal events: A refutation of Nisbett and Wilson and of Bem. *Psychological Review,* 1980, *87,* 105-112.

White, R. W. Motivation reconsidered: The concept of competence. *Psychological Review,* 1959, *66,* 297-333.

Wicklund, R. A. *Freedom and reactance.* Hillsdale, N.J.: Lawrence Erlbaum Associates, 1974.

Wong, P. T. P., & Weiner, B. When people ask why questions and the temporal course of the attribution process. Unpublished manuscript, 1979.

Worchel, S., & Andreoli, V. A. Attribution of causality as a means of restoring behavioral freedom. *Journal of Personality and Social Psychology,* 1974, *29,* 237-245.

Worchel, S., & Cooper, J. *Understanding social psychology* (Revised edition). Homewood, Ill.: Dorsey, 1979.

Wortman, C. B. Some determinants of perceived control. *Journal of Personality and Social Psychology,* 1975, *31,* 282–294.

Wortman, C. B., & Brehm, J. W. Responses to uncontrollable outcomes: An integration of reactance theory and the learned helplessness model. In L. Berkowitz (Ed.), *Advances in experimental social psychology* (Vol. 8). New York: Academic Press, 1975.

Wyer, R. S. An information-processing perspective on social attribution. In J. H. Harvey, W. Ickes, & R. F. Kidd (Eds.), *New directions in attribution research* (Vol. 3). Hillsdale, N.J.: Lawrence Erlbaum Associates, in press.

Wyer, R. S., & Carlston, D. E. *Social cognition, inference and attribution.* Hillsdale, N.J.: Lawrence Erlbaum Associates, 1979.

Yarkin, K. L., Harvey, J. H., & Bloxom, B. M. Cognitive sets, attribution, and social interaction. *Journal of Personality and Social Psychology: Attitudes and Social Cognition,* in press.

Zillman, D. Attribution and misattribution of excitatory reactions. In J. H. Harvey, W. J. Ickes, & R. F. Kidd (Eds.), *New directions in attribution research* (Vol. 2). Hillsdale, N.J.: Lawrence Erlbaum Associates, 1978.

Zillman, D., & Cantor, J. R. Effect of timing of information about mitigating circumstances on emotional responses to provocation and retaliatory behavior. *Journal of Experimental Social Psychology,* 1976, *12,* 38–55.

Zuckerman, M. Attribution of success and failure revisited, or: The motivational bias is alive and well in attribution theory. *Journal of Personality,* 1979, *47,* 245–287.

Zuckerman, M. On the endogenous-exogenous partition in attribution theory. *Personality and Social Psychology Bulletin,* 1977, *3,* 389–399.

Zuckerman, M., & Lubin, B. *Manual for the Multiple Affect Adjective Check List.* San Diego, Calif.: Educational and Industrial Testing Service, 1965.

Author Index

Subject Index